WALKING
SAN DIEGO

Where to Go to Get Away from It All

WALKING SAN DIEGO

Where to Go to Get Away from It All

SECOND EDITION

Lonnie Burstein Hewitt
Barbara Coffin Moore

THE
MOUNTAINEERS
BOOKS

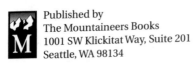

Published by
The Mountaineers Books
1001 SW Klickitat Way, Suite 201
Seattle, WA 98134

First edition, 1989
Second edition: first printing 2000, second printing 2002

Published simultaneously in Great Britain by Cordee, 3a DeMontfort Street, Leicester, England, LE1 7HD

Manufactured in the United States of America

Managing Editor: Kathleen Cubley
Editor: Jane Crosen
Designer and Layout Artist: Kristy L. Welch
Maps by Jo P. Griffith, Jerry Painter, and Tina Matthias
All photographs by Susan Green unless otherwise noted

Cover photograph: *Torrey Pine in California* © Jan Butchofsky/Corbis
Frontispiece: *Lake Jennings* © Susan Green

Library of Congress Cataloging-in-Publication Data

Hewitt, Lonnie Burstein, 1942-
       Walking San Diego : where to go to get away from it all / Lonnie
Burstein Hewitt and Barbara Coffin Moore.— 2nd ed.
          p.   cm.
       Includes bibliographical references (p.   ) and index.
       ISBN 0-89886-692-8
       1. Walking—California—San Diego—Guidebooks. 2.
Hiking—California—San Diego—Guidebooks. 3. San Diego
(Calif.)—Guidebooks. I. Moore, Barbara Coffin, 1939- II. Title.
GV199.42.C22 S264 2000
917.94'9850454—dc21   00-009224
                                           CIP

To our fathers,

who would have enjoyed these walks

■ ■ ■

Contents

part III **WALKING SHORTS**
A Bundle of Extras for More Walking Pleasure

Acknowledgments

Walking San Diego has been a big part of our lives for more than a year, and many people have helped to make it possible. We'd like to thank the park rangers, city and county officials, naturalists, and historians who gave us hours of their time and interest, with special thanks to the very knowledgeable Hank Nicol, for reviewing the entire manuscript. Thanks to our photographer, Susan R. Green; our mapmaker, Jo P. Griffith; and our artists, Kathryn Watson and David Stump; for their invaluable contributions. Thanks to our families, friends, students, and associates for putting up with our monomania, to all the walkers, cyclists, and horseback riders who answered our questions on the trails, and to Maurice Hewitt, husband and friend, for help and encouragement beyond the call of duty.

Acknowledgments 2000. Many thanks to Tina Matthias for updating our maps, Elaine Steele for copy editing assistance, and Kathy Estey for checking the numbers. Thanks to the rangers and park managers who answered our innumerable questions: Pam Baughman, Chris Sargent-Beach, Gerald Burton, Jake Enriquez, Rick Felchlin, Judy Good, Nancy Hansen, Lori Hynes, Phil Jenkens, Beth Jensen, Craig Julene, Isabelle Kaye, Diane Kennedy, Paul Kucharczyk, Nola Lamkin, Bill Lawrence, David Martinez, Belinda Romero, Tom Roster, Barbara Simon, Shannon Smith, Tracy Walker, Susan Welker, and Bob Wohl.

Authors at work, then. . .

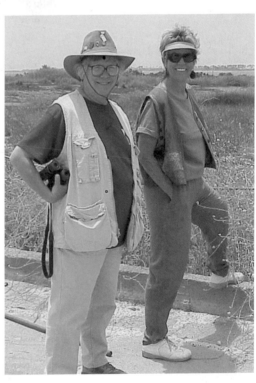

and now

Authors' Note

Once a small town with a military air, San Diego is today the fastest-growing area in California. More than 32 million people visit here every year, and many of them never leave. At the turn of the twenty-first century the countywide population is 2.7 million. San Diego is now the fifth largest city in the country.

Rapid growth has brought new problems. Air and water quality are not what they used to be, and sometimes freeway traffic is uncomfortably like L.A.'s. Our hillsides have been stripped, flattened, and covered with buildings; the wide open spaces have virtually disappeared.

But there are still a surprising number of lovely and little-known places where you can find a quiet spot for a hike, a picnic, or just a breath of traffic-free air—even on a summer Sunday.

Here are some of our favorites, enough for months of outings. We've tried to point you in the best directions, and tell you about the plants, birds, and animals you'll see along the way. We've included some local history, as many odd and interesting facts as we could fit in, and still kept the whole thing easy to read and carry. You can count on doing some walking, but nothing strenuous; most of our walks are about two hours long, suitable for all ages, and less than an hour's drive from downtown.

We've had such fun collecting material for *Walking San Diego* we can't wait to share it. Once you start exploring the trails for yourself, we think you'll see what we mean. These are places to return to again and again, with every season a little bit different and every visit a new adventure.

If you have any additions or suggestions, please let us hear from you. Meanwhile, happy trails!

Lonnie & Barbara

June 2000: Ten years after our first edition, a surprising number of our original sites are still looking good. We've changed what's outdated and added more than twenty new walks, enough to keep you and your family busy for the next ten years. We wish you a happy new century, and look forward to seeing you out on the trail!

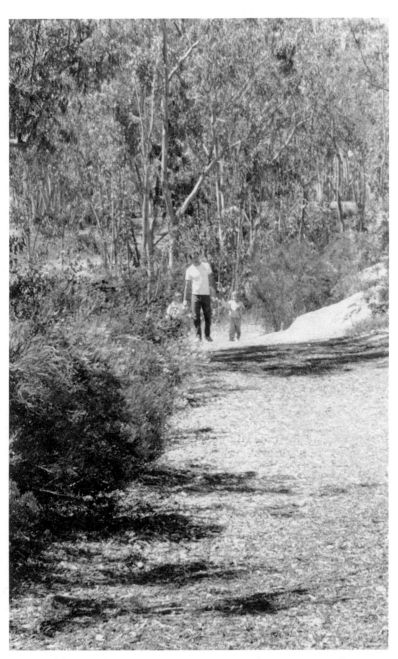

Sunday in the park

A Word to the Walker

Some of the walks in this book are strolls; some are more like hikes. All of them can be done by anyone in reasonably good physical condition, without any special hiking skills.

It's best to wear cushioned running or walking shoes, comfortable ones with a decent tread, so you don't lose your grip on the road. A walking stick can be useful too, especially on hills; it's always nice to have an extra leg to stand on.

Walking is great exercise, and a brisk walk uphill can be just as good a cardiovascular workout as jogging, without the shin splints and back strain. But walking briskly often means you miss a lot of what we're walking for—the sights and sounds of our natural environment.

We usually figure on a 20- to 30-minute flat mile, taking plenty of time to smell the flowers. If you want more action, try pumping your arms as you walk, like a sprinter. Breathe deeply. Smile! It's not just the exercise, but the sense of well-being that comes from an hour or two spent on your own two feet in the fresh, fume-less air that really does your heart good!

Though we think all our trails are safe and not terribly strenuous, a normal amount of caution is advised. Stay on the marked trails; shortcuts can be dangerous to you and the wildlife you trample. Watch your step on rocky paths, and on wet ones, where things can get slippery. It goes without saying that children especially should be watched carefully, particularly around cliffs and canyons.

Times being what they are, it's not such a great idea to go walking alone. If you don't have a regular walking companion, ask around, advertise in your local paper, or join a group. There's safety in numbers, and it's nice to share your discoveries.

The Natural History Museum's Canyoneers, the Audubon Society, Walkabout, and other organizations frequently offer guided walks. Check the outdoor activities or weekend section of your newspaper.

WHAT TO WEAR, WHAT TO CARRY

Next to walking or running shoes, sun visors are our most valued piece of attire. Even if you're caught in the rain, a visor can help keep your glasses dry. On rougher trails, long pants protect you from the shrubbery and any leg-loving insects.

Here's a suggestion of what you might want to bring along, remembering, of course, that he (or she) travels best who travels light. A small day pack should carry everything you could possibly want or need and still leave your hands free for your walking stick, binoculars, camera, or notepad.

- Sunscreen, especially in summer
- Binoculars for viewing birds and distant flowers
- Notepad and pen for notes and plant sketches
- Sweater or windbreaker for unexpected weather changes
- Camera
- Bandaids and antiseptic, just in case
- Snacks or picnic lunch
- A small water bottle (Hot tip: Put your water bottle in the freezer the night before; don't fill it too full or it will crack. This gives you ice water for hot-day hikes.)

Actually, we keep a few essentials in the back of the car: an extra pair of socks and sneakers, a jacket, a walking stick, and a sun visor. That way, we're always ready!

WEATHER OR NOT

San Diego's reputation as a place of year-round perfect weather is a little misleading. Generally speaking, we don't have four seasons, but two: winter/wet and summer/dry. But some years are wetter than others, with destructive storms flooding beach towns and valleys, and some are bone-dry, draining our reservoirs.

Depending on how much rain there's been, spring wildflowers may come out in January or April. September and October are often the hottest months, and summer may be no summer at all, especially along the coast, which can be damp, cool, and foggy, while inland temperatures soar into the 90s. Winter can bring snow to the mountains, but anywhere else, it's highly unlikely. Any time of year, mornings and evenings can be chilly; 30-degree swings in temperature are not unusual.

What all this means is—be prepared. The layered look is always appropriate: a sweater on top of a long-sleeved shirt on top of a short-sleeved one. Then you're covered—or uncovered—no matter what weather comes up.

Unhappily, smog has made its way to San Diego, and it can be a real irritant to some walkers, causing breathing difficulty, stinging eyes, and other allergic symptoms. In early fall, the hot desert winds called Santa Anas blow pollutants out to sea, but as the winds weaken, a southward drift takes over, and we end up with a swirl of smog from L.A. If you're sensitive, you'll feel it long before smog alerts are announced. For a report on the latest conditions, call Air Pollution Control at (858) 565-6626.

Since weather can vary greatly from day to day and place to place, you might want to check with the weather bureau before deciding which way to go. You can get a comprehensive, countywide forecast anytime by calling (858) 289-1212.

TRAIL DO'S AND DON'TS

Don't take living souvenirs. Nearly all our sites are protected, and none of them could stand the strain of every visitor picking just one little wildflower.

Don't take our mention of Indian usages of plants for an endorsement. Don't taste anything you're not absolutely sure you know.

Don't forget: "Leaves of three, let it be." Learn how to recognize poison oak in all seasons, and keep out of it (see Appendix A).

Don't tease any animal, or pet anything that doesn't belong to you. Wildlife should be admired, and treated with respect. Keep an eye out for rattlesnakes (see sidebar), especially in springtime.

Los Peñasquitos Canyon

A Word About Snakes

Of all the county's thirty-three species of snakes, rattlesnakes are the only ones to be concerned about. Easily recognized by their triangular heads and the warning rattles at the end of their tails, they're wonderful to watch—from a safe distance.

Members of the pit viper family, rattlesnakes have heat-sensitive pits on each side of their heads, which help them sense the presence of mice or gophers in the dark and human walkers in the daytime. Like us, they want to avoid confrontation. The greatest danger is stepping on a sleeping snake: abruptly awakened, it's likely to strike first and rattle a warning later.

All snakes are cold-blooded animals that need to be warm to digest their food. A cold snake can actually die of indigestion. That's why they're most frequently seen in spring, stretched out in the sun after a meal. Snakes in Southern California don't hibernate in winter, as they do in colder climates; whenever it's warm enough, they do their hunting and digesting at night.

If you should see a rattlesnake, just back away slowly; it will probably do the same. Don't yell, wave your arms, or try to frighten the snake; you'll only confuse it.

If worse comes to worst, and you do get bitten, don't panic. Tie a constrictive band 4 to 6 inches above the bite; don't tie it too tightly, and don't apply ice. If you're out in the middle of nowhere, start walking slowly back toward civilization. The best remedy for snakebite is your car key. Head for the nearest hospital; antivenin is available throughout the county. For more information, call the Poison Control Center at (800) 876-4766.

Rattlesnake (left), Gopher Snake (right)

A Note About Safety

Safety is an important concern in all outdoor activities. No guidebook can alert you to every hazard or anticipate the limitations of every reader, so the descriptions in this book are not representations that a particular trip is safe for your party. When you take a trip, you assume responsibility for your own safety. Some of the trips described in this book may require you to do no more than look both ways before crossing the street; on others, more attention to safety may be required due to terrain, traffic, weather, the capabilities of your party, or other factors. Keeping informed on current conditions and exercising common sense are the keys to a safe, enjoyable outing.

The Mountaineers Books

Last but not least—do we have to say it?—don't litter. Trashing our wild spaces will leave us nothing worth walking in. As city trash can signs once said: Every Litter Bit Hurts.

Lest we start sounding too negative, here are some do's: Do take time to look for animal tracks, listen to a bird's song, or admire a tiny flower. That's what *Walking San Diego* is all about. Just giving the area a once-over glance, you might miss such camouflaged creatures as the horned lizard, one of our favorites.

Do feel free to do half a walk, or less, or more, as the spirit moves you. Scribble in the book, add your personal notes, make it your own.

And please, do enjoy yourself. We mean these walks to be fun!

A WORD ABOUT THE BOOK

Walking San Diego is as user-friendly as we could make it. Dip in wherever you like, depending on where you want to go; you don't have to read it in order.

The "TG numbers" at each location refer to the Thomas Guide 2000, which many San Diegans swear by. The page number is followed by map coordinates. For more information, here are some useful websites:

California State Parks, *cal-parks.ca.gov/travel/regions/sandiego*

San Diego City Parks, *www.ci.san-diego.ca.us/park-and-recreation/parks*

San Diego County Parks, *www.co.san-diego.ca.us/parks*

City Lakes, *www.sdfish.com*

Please Note: We do our best to stay current, but hours, trails, and admission fees are subject to change. To avoid disappointment, remember: **Call first.**

Kumeyaay mother and child
(Photo courtesy of the Mountain Empire Historical Society)

San Diego, Then and Now

In the days when dinosaurs still roamed the earth, San Diego was a series of volcanic islands, mostly under water. As the seas receded, the islands rose, becoming mountains. Over millions of years, they were worn down by the elements into masses of sediment that formed a great coastal plain.

About 22 million years ago, this coastal plain was jolted by seismic activity and resurfaced as new mountain ranges extending from Los Angeles into Baja California.

San Diego was probably a more wooded place, and warmer, when the earliest human inhabitants arrived about 10,000 years ago. They were stone-age hunters, following herds of large and edible animals—mammoths, bison, and saber-toothed tigers—across the bridge of land from Asia to Alaska, and down the coast. Apart from some crude stone tools, they left few relics of their existence. As one of their key sites was along what the Spanish called the San Dieguito River, they are sometimes referred to as the San Dieguito culture.

Next on the scene were the La Jollans, who settled near coastal lagoons where fish and shellfish were plentiful. Though archaeologists once assumed they had succeeded the San Dieguito people, more recent discoveries show they may have lived here at about the same time. Whether they were part of the same culture or another one is still open to question.

The last group of "Indians"—Columbus' misnomer that blankets all the original inhabitants of the New World—came westward from the Colorado River Valley about 1200 years ago. They knew how to use bows and arrows, make pottery, and gather a wide variety of plants for food, including acorns, which they laboriously ground into meal. They were still here when the Spanish came, changed their lives, obliterated their culture, and named them Diegueños after the mission built to oversee their conversion. Those north of the San Diego River called themselves Ipai; south of the river were the Tipai, or Kumeyaay.

The generations of Indians who lived in the area pretty much took their natural surroundings as they found them. They lived in simple brushwood shelters, gathering what they could in season and storing the surplus for emergencies. Where there were pine trees, they gathered pine nuts. Where there were berries, they ate them, raw or cooked. When a deer or a rabbit crossed their path, they killed it with a throwing stick, used its skin for clothing, and shared its meat with their extended family. In summer, when streams dried up, they went to surer water sources in the mountains, where their favorite acorn-bearing oaks were found. They lived in harmony with

Threshing bee at the Antique Gas and Steam Engine Museum at Guajome Regional Park
(Photo courtesy of the Antique Gas and Steam Engine Museum)

nature, finding nutritional, medicinal, or other uses for almost everything they encountered.

European arrivals saw things differently. Nature was meant to be tamed. Wherever they settled, they tried to make it look like where they had come from, importing plants and animals, building houses that resembled the ones they left behind. They didn't just want to adapt and survive, as the Kumeyaay had. They wanted to change their surroundings to suit their taste.

Before the Spanish came in 1769, there were no horses, cattle, or sheep, and nothing that we would call cultivation, though Kumeyaay knew how to burn an area to make it produce more abundantly the following year (see the sidebar "A Word About Chaparral" in Chapter 2).

Spanish missionaries supervised the building of the first dam and aqueduct, so they could water the wheat, olives, grapes, corn, and beans they had planted. In the quarter century of Mexican rule, the new native *Californios*, Spanish descendants, established huge ranchos where they raised range cattle. The hides—"California banknotes"—became San Diego's most profitable export.

After the Mexican War of 1846–47, California became U.S. territory. Once the Americans took over San Diego, they started developing it in ways the Spanish had never dreamed of—railroads, subdivisions, resorts, and freeways. The rivers, dammed practically out of existence, no longer flowed freely to the sea. Unable to replenish their sands, beaches eroded, and run-off ate away the bluffs that had been here for millions of years. Pollution, the by-product of civilization, started taking its toll on plant and animal life; only by concerted effort could endangered species be saved.

Today, most of the things we take for granted here come from some-where else. The water that turns a near-desert into a place of green lawns and tropical flowers is nearly 90 percent imported, from the Colorado River and Northern California. Oranges, originally Asian, were brought from Spain via Mexico. Avocados are Central American; eucalyptus trees, Australian. Our three main natural habitats—chaparral, wetlands, and stream-side—have been invaded by "foreigners" who have made themselves at home, even as the rest of us non-native San Diegans have done.

As you follow our trails, consider how the area might have looked be-fore Junipero Serra, Alonzo Horton, John D. Spreckels, Colonel Ed Fletcher, or the Scripps family came to town. Our open spaces are a blend of the natural and the civilized, what nature has supplied, and what man has added to it. They are themselves fragile things, and your considerate use and support will help assure their continued existence.

Part I

COASTAL
SAN DIEGO

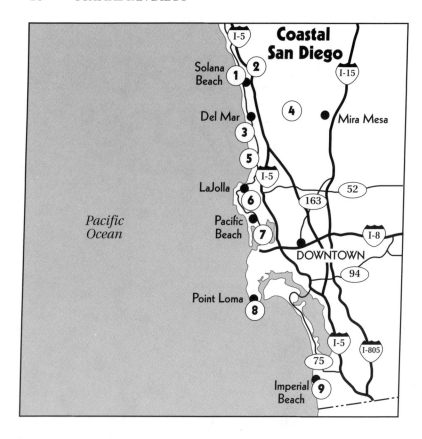

1 SAN ELIJO LAGOON ECOLOGICAL RESERVE

LOCATION
Solana Beach.

For West Basin, Walks 1 and 2: From I-5, take Lomas Santa Fe Drive west about 1 mile to North Rios Avenue. Turn right and park at the end. (TG1167:E6).

For East Basin, Walks 3 and 4: Take Lomas Santa Fe Drive east to Santa Helena, just after the freeway overpass. Turn left. Then turn left again on Santa Victoria, and make one more left on Santa Carina, across from the school. Park at the end of the street (TG1167:H5).

HOURS
Sunrise to sunset.

DESCRIPTION

San Elijo Lagoon is a 1000-acre wildlife reserve that is owned by the California Department of Fish and Game and the county, and is popular with migratory and nesting waterfowl. Two hundred and seventy species of birds have been counted here, making the area a favorite of birders. Two man-made islands in the east basin provide safe places to nest, with the water level controlled to inhibit access by coyotes, snakes, and other predators. There are many different walks you can take in the reserve, with plant life ranging from subtropical to wetlands to chaparral. A small visitor center on the northwest shore, off Manchester Avenue, has the only restrooms. Guided walks are available by calling (760) 436-3944.

A Word About Wetlands

Wetlands are low-lying marshy areas that connect inland waterways to the sea. Unlike East Coast wetlands, Southern California's are generally dry in summer, and wet only when inundated by high tides, storms, or local runoff.

San Diego's coastal wetlands are primarily places of brackish water—an ever-changing mixture of saltwater and fresh—that support a tremendous variety of wildlife. Our bays, lagoons, mudflats, and salt marshes provide rest stops and winter homes for more than 100 species of migratory birds, and comfortable habitats for nesting ones. At low tide, thousands of these birds converge on the mudflats to make a meal of some of the crabs, clams, shrimps, snails, and worms that live there. Wetlands are also an important spawning ground for many ocean-dwelling fish, and in stormy season, they help control flooding by acting as a buffer between the waves and the higher uplands.

But, for all their usefulness, they are little appreciated. More than 90 percent of our coastal wetlands are gone forever, dredged for harbors and marinas; filled for airports, highways, and railroads; developed into sites for hotels, power plants, shipyards, and shopping centers; diked for salt production; polluted by urban and agricultural runoff; choked by sediments from construction sites; and killed by upstream dams.

Some of Southern California's best remaining wetland areas can be found along the San Diego coast. Avid birders love these areas, but there's plenty to interest the casual walker too.

HISTORY

For thousands of years, the area around San Elijo was inhabited by Kumeyaay. All along the shores are seashell middens, or trash heaps, containing the remains of scallops, clams, and other shellfish no longer found here, since very little seawater comes into the lagoon anymore.

Until the 1880s, the lagoon had fairly good access to the ocean. Those were the days of wide, sandy beaches, with no barriers to block the flow of sand or water.

The coming of the railroad changed all that. Trains had to have a dry, level road to run on, so a raised levee was built across the lagoon and the course of its feeder creek was altered. This was the first step in turning a self-sufficient wetland into one that needed human intervention in order to survive.

In the 1920s, San Elijo became a kind of open cesspool, used for settling sewage. In the late 1960s, when the I-5 freeway split it in two, the lagoon was left with no way to flush itself clean. Only the bulldozers brought in from time to time to clear its silt-clogged mouth keep San Elijo from stagnating completely.

Until the 1970s, when it was acquired by the county and made into an ecological reserve, the lagoon was popular with duck hunters. ·

Uplands on both north and south shores have been farmed for years. In the early part of the century, drought-tolerant lima beans were the major crop; today, strawberries and trendy oriental vegetables are grown on the north side of Manchester Avenue. Although the lands here are not part of the reserve, the use of chemical pesticides and fertilizers may be a real threat to the well-being of the lagoon and its wildlife.

WEST BASIN

Walk 1—The Jungle Trail (Gemma Parks Trail)
Distance: 1.7 miles round trip. *Time:* 45 minutes to 1 hour.

If you think our local plant life is dry, brown, and scrubby, this walk should change your mind. It's a piece of tropical rainforest in the midst of coastal chaparral, a ferny little wilderness between the wetlands and the new developments, named for local environmental activist Gemma Parks.

Begin your walk on the south side of the lagoon, where North Rios Avenue dead-ends near luxury homes with expansive (and expensive) views from the mountains to the sea.

Walking downhill to the right, you'll find a stand of castor bean trees, whose broad-leafed branches overhang the path. Most of the year, you can see their large flower clusters and bristly red seed pods. Sometimes called the deadliest seeds on earth, no two of the intricately marked beans are alike.

As poisonous as they are, an amazing variety of products has been derived from their oil; in fact, castor oil itself is one of man's earliest commercial products. Formerly used as lamp oil and given regularly to constipated children, it is now used in high-performance engines and as a main ingredient in soaps, inks, cosmetics, plastics, nylon, paints and varnishes, insulation materials, and brake and embalming fluids. The toxin, ricin, is currently being studied as a promising cure for cancer.

The sun rarely reaches this part of the trail, so it's often damp and sometimes downright muddy. In summer, you'll notice distinct changes of humidity as you move from shaded to open areas. In spring, there's such a profusion of pastel wild radish you might think you're in an English country garden. There are also patches of orange and yellow nasturtiums, "escaped" from neighborhood gardens years ago, when people started dumping their cuttings here.

You may catch a whiff of licorice in the air before you see the tall stalks of fennel, with its ferny leaves. It is said that the padres scattered fennel on the floors of their chapels so it would perfume the air when crushed by the weight of kneeling—and certainly unwashed—supplicants. The seeds taste of licorice too, and are often served in East Indian restaurants as an after-dinner breath freshener. If you can't smell the licorice right off, try rubbing the leaves between your fingers.

This licorice smell is one of the big differences between fennel and its deadly look-alike, poison hemlock. Hemlock killed Socrates, and has done in a number of grazing cattle. There have been a few cases of humans dying too, after eating hemlock seeds mistaken for fennel, or trying the old Boy Scout trick of making whistles out of the hollow stalks. Poison hemlock leaves look more like carrot tops than ferns, but in winter, when both plants are dry, seed-topped stalks, the difference is harder to notice. There are a number of hemlock plants growing around the lagoon too, so unless you're absolutely positive you know what you're tasting, DON'T.

This applies equally to any mushrooms that you may find along the trail, especially after it rains. Some years ago, two Northern California students cooked, ate, and enjoyed some mushrooms they had collected; one ended up having to have a liver transplant. It's safer to look, but don't touch; some of the mushrooms here have really interesting shapes and colors.

Winter is the best time to see the profusion of bright green polypody ferns along the north-facing slopes of the path. Ferns, the descendants of ancient water plants, are usually found in moist areas. In spring, you can feel rows of tiny lumps on the backs of the fronds. These are the spores, which grow into new plants that don't look like adult ferns at all. Eventually, the almost invisible offspring produce sperm and eggs; each fertilized egg becomes a new fern. Like all of San Diego's twenty-six native ferns, polypody sprouts after the first fall rains, and by June is completely dried up.

The jungly part of the trail is short, but sweet. Afterwards, you'll emerge into the more typical coastal sage scrub: buckwheat, sagebrush, and sage. This was a jeep road until the early 1980s, when a heavy rainstorm sent the whole hillside sliding down in the kind of instant erosion geologists call "slope slump."

Notice the arroyo willows on the lagoon side of the trail. If you come here between January and March, you should be able to find furry "pussy willows," chartreuse catkins, yellow flowers, and fluff-covered seeds, all on the same tree. Actually, you can tell the sex of a willow by the color of its catkins—yellow for fellows, green for girls. Also in this area are acacia trees, flaunting their sneeze-provoking yellow blossoms in late winter and early spring.

Beyond the trees is a sandy clearing formed by runoff from overwatered hilltop lawns. From here, follow the lower Shoreside Trail left, if you want to observe some of the water birds that make their home in the lagoon. You'll usually find a number of white-billed black coots swimming around; some people call them mud hens. Watch for their fluffy multicolored chicks in summer.

In winter, when hundreds of migratory water birds arrive, try to distinguish the two groups of ducks: dabblers and divers. The dabblers—redheads, pintails, shovelers, and mallards—are the ones you usually see with their tails in the air, feeding off the shallow bottom. The divers—scaup, ruddy ducks, and buffleheads—are the ones that disappear into the deeper water to search for food.

Other swimmers worth watching are the tailless pied-billed grebes. In summer, they carry their babies on their backs and sink out of sight like

San Elijo Lagoon

submarines. Note the variety of shorebirds too: pink-legged stilts, avocets with their upcurved bills, gray willets, brown dowitchers whose beaks peck through the mud with the speed of sewing machine needles, and the beautiful long-legged waders—great blue herons, white egrets, and the iridescent black white-faced ibis.

When it rains, this lower trail may flood out, but you can usually bypass the flooded areas. There are several kinds of salt marsh plants here, even though the water is not very salty anymore. Notice the pickleweed, a low-growing succulent with tiny pickle-shaped leaves that turn red in fall. In March, in the shallows around the pickleweed, watch for the frantic activity of spawning carp, some of them 2 feet long.

The Shoreside Trail meets up with the main trail which goes straight through the chaparral—mostly broom, deerweed, and sagebrush. From here, you can continue east up to the freeway embankment, then head north (left), finally crossing under the freeway to the west end of Walk 3.

We like to take the trail that forks to the right, heading back through the trees of the Vanishing Forest, a grove of eucalyptus, acacia, mimosa, palms, and Monterey cypress, planted years ago as ornamentals. As time and storms take their toll, dead trees are replaced with native cottonwoods, live oaks, and willows by rangers and some of the volunteers who are actively involved in the reserve's maintenance and preservation. There are a number of offshoot paths that lead in and around the trees; look carefully, and you'll find the foundations of an old farmhouse that once stood here.

On your left, past the wooded area, is a place we call The Meadow. In spring, the slopes here are covered with golden California poppies, yellow sea dahlias, blue lupine, red paintbrush, and the picturesquely named Chinese houses. Resist the temptation to take home a bouquet; remember, this is a protected area.

Continuing west along the Upper Trail, you'll see a path uphill into Holmwood Canyon. About 0.1 mile up is an attractive rest stop under a spreading eucalyptus tree, with a stone bench commemorating the life and work of Gemma Parks. If you don't take this detour, in a few minutes you'll come to the jungle again, and be heading back to your car.

Walk 2—The Pole Road Trail
Distance: 1.5 miles. *Time:* 45 minutes to 1 hour.

This walk is especially favored by birders, because it gives them a chance to get close to many of the birds that winter in the lagoon. From the Rios entrance, follow the dirt road down toward the water, take the path that forks to the right, and go out onto the Isthmus, a levee in the middle of the lagoon.

The higher areas that birds like to rest on are the remnants of the old sewage dikes; when the water level is low, you can see their hourglass shape. The posts occupied by terns, gulls, and cormorants mark underground gas and sewage pipelines.

There are always ducks here, and usually hawks, great blue herons, and pelicans. In early summer, you can't miss the stilts and avocets, who fly at you, shrieking, trying to frighten you away from their nests.

Return to the dirt road and follow it to the gravel Pole Road used by San Diego Gas and Electric to maintain its powerlines. From here, you can go north, almost all the way to Cardiff.

As you walk on by, you may notice the telltale scent of the cement block pumping station; take shallow breaths and try to ignore it. Look for green-backed herons fishing along the shore and kingfishers perched on the powerlines. Continue past the old sewage treatment plant, where we once took shelter during a sudden downpour. At the end, above and to the right of the railroad trestle, are the remains of an old kelp factory, which, during World War I, produced kelp by-products used in the manufacture of gunpowder.

EAST BASIN

Walks 3 and 4 begin at the north end of Santa Carina, east of I-5. Cross through the old lima bean fields, now covered with broom and other chaparral shrubs. You'll begin to see bits of broken shell underfoot, the scattered remains of ancient Indian seafood feasts, from the days when shellfish were still plentiful here. Leavings were heaped up and covered with dirt, before the smell became overpowering. Farmers clearing the land disturbed these kitchen middens in the early part of this century. Now walkers and gophers are uncovering them again. The origin of the bits of shell along the freeway embankment is less certain; they're part of the landfill, and might have come from anywhere.

The path forks at about 0.2 mile, near two large eucalyptus trees. Walk 3 heads west toward the freeway, and Walk 4 heads east to El Camino Real.

Walk 3—Tern Point and Flood Control Dike
Distance: 2 miles round trip. *Time:* 45 minutes to 1 hour.

When you come to the eucalyptus trees, take the left-forking trail. There are several dead trees here that are hunting perches for kites, hawks, kingbirds, woodpeckers, and ravens, so keep your eyes open. Stay on the upper trail that leads out to Tern Point, and you'll have a good view of the entire east basin and the two islands, where avocets, killdeer, mallards, and the endangered least terns make their nests during the summer. Biologists have placed red roof tiles on the islands to provide shade for the least tern chicks.

Retrace your steps back to the main trail, heading west toward the freeway. Up ahead on the left is a deep gully, evidence of erosion by overwatered lawns on the street above.

Notice how the chaparral plant community comes right down to meet the salt marsh. If you keep your eyes on the edge of the cattails, just at water level, you might see a Virginia rail or an American bittern, shy birds that live among the reeds.

If you continue toward the freeway, you can pick up the trail that goes along the embankment and under the overpass to connect with Walk 1, the Jungle Trail.

When the water level is low enough, you can cross the flood control dike to Manchester Avenue. Look for the tracks of raccoons in the mud, and the leftover claws of their crayfish dinners. This is another good place for birding; great blue herons and egrets like to sit on the fence waiting for a catfish, carp, or bass to swim by. You may even see a sharp-eyed osprey dive down into the water, and fly back up to a feeding perch, holding its catch like a torpedo.

Walk 4—La Orilla Trail
Distance: 2 miles round trip. *Time:* 45 minutes to 1 hour.

Just past the north end of Santa Carina, take the right fork near the eucalyptus trees and head east toward the powerlines. Soon you'll start going downhill, past a hillside thickly covered with fuchsia-flowered gooseberry, scrub oak, bush monkey flower, cucumber vines, honeysuckle, and chaparral pea. The lagoon side of the path will give you a glimpse of many of the visiting waterfowl. One foggy morning, we saw a well-fed coyote watching for birds—just like us.

About 0.5 mile along the trail, you'll reach a flatter area where there are clumps of pale pampas grass. Introduced in the late 1800s, when huge urns full of the tall plumes were part of every fashionable Victorian drawing room, pampas grass is another escaped plant that spreads quickly and suffocates its neighbors. Digging out these clumps is a back-breaking job, but the Parks Department is getting county prisoners to do the work, which may go a long way toward convincing them that crime doesn't pay.

There are large stretches of pickleweed around here, home to the endangered savannah sparrow. In June, you'll see the showy yellow blossoms of Hooker's evening primrose, named for a botanist friend of Darwin, not a lady of easy virtue. In fall, look for goldfinches digging out seeds from the dead flower clusters.

Past the powerlines, La Orilla Trail meanders through a sandy section and finally merges with a horse trail through the marshland called Orilla Creek. The Parks Department has improved the trail, leading it to somewhat higher and drier ground, where pink alkali heath and yellow daisy-like salty susan bloom in summer. You can continue east to El Camino Real, the old Indian trail followed by Spanish soldiers and missionaries on their travels north. We love the shady eucalyptus groves here; for a nice variation, start your walk from this end, parking near the corner of La Orilla and El Camino Real.

2 SAN DIEGUITO PARK

LOCATION

Solana Beach/Rancho Santa Fe. From I-5, take the Lomas Santa Fe exit and go east about 1 mile (TG1167:J6).

Upper Entrance: From Lomas Santa Fe, go north on Highland Drive. Turn right, then left into park.

Lower Entrance: From Lomas Santa Fe, go north on Highland Drive to El Camino Real. Turn right; the entrance is 200 yards ahead on the right.

HOURS

9:30 A.M. to sunset. Parking fee.

DESCRIPTION

This 122-acre oasis in fast-growing North County is a great place to go for a family picnic, a morning run, or a quiet stroll. It's a combination of developed and "natural" attractions, including a ballfield, horseshoe pits and playgrounds, picnic tables and barbecues, and an equestrian trail. Although much of the park is on hilly ground, there is handicapped access to picnic areas and restrooms. Group picnic areas, a paved dancing pavilion, and the grassy slope beside the Wedding Pond may be reserved for private parties. A youth-group campsite is also available. Call County Parks, (858) 694-3049, for reservations.

HISTORY

San Dieguito, "Little San Diego," was the name of a rancho established here by the first mayor of the pueblo of San Diego, Juan Maria Osuna. The area had been designated as an Indian settlement in the 1830s when Governor Figueroa started "secularizing" the missions, but Osuna, not bothering with the fine points, simply appropriated 8000 acres of the best land, acquiring a formal grant in 1845.

When he died, the rancho was inherited by his son, Leandro, who treated the Indians like slaves. They retaliated by feeding him a concoction of cactus fruit and ground human bones, reputed to cause a slow and painful death. Believing he was doomed, Leandro shot himself; some say his ghost still wanders the grounds of San Dieguito.

In 1906, a branch of the Santa Fe Railroad Company bought up all the original property and renamed it Rancho Santa Fe. Executives envisioning forests of cheap railroad ties imported three million eucalyptus seedlings from Australia. Fast-growing, drought-tolerant, and very much in vogue, eucalyptus turned out to be a disappointment; the wood warped when wet and split as soon as they drove a spike into it. The project was abandoned, but the trees remain, tall and silent witnesses to the dangers of insufficient research. Hummingbirds and orioles seem to love them anyway.

The Walk

Distance: 1.5 miles round trip. *Time:* 45 minutes to 1 hour.

Our favorite hike starts at the lower entrance. Drive in, bear left, and park just south of the restrooms. You'll pass a pair of duck ponds, a popular hangout for what birders call "funny ducks," the half-breed offspring of wild mallards and abandoned domestic ones. Some of them will swim right up to visitors, looking for a handout; carry along a few slices of bread if you want to feed them. You can always tell the wild mallards—they're the ones that ignore you. Some days, you may also see a kingfisher, an egret, or a great blue heron.

From the ponds, you get a fine view of the broad green slopes and the variety of trees found in the lower part of the park. There are sycamores, black willows, pepper trees, pomegranates, liquid ambar—a red maple look-alike—and, of course, eucalyptus.

Once you've had a general look around, walk up the main road. About 100 yards from the second drainage crossing, you'll come to a dirt road on your right, with an "Authorized Vehicles Only" sign. Follow it uphill, bearing right. If you smell something sweet, it's Cleveland sage; there's a small clump on the mound where the trail forks at the top.

Still bearing right, stay on the main trail, heading toward a single tall eucalyptus. You'll see a yellow ridge of Torrey sandstone, slowly shaped under shallow seas millions of years ago and eroded by wind and rain when the water receded. There's a good vista point here, with views from the huge homes and horse paddocks of Rancho Santa Fe all the way to the mountains.

You are now on Activity Hill, an imaginative play area for children and—why not?—playful adults. Start with the bouncy swinging bridge to your right, cross the second bridge, and go on to the double log balance beams. Heading back up to the top are three big ladders; farther down is a single log balance beam. Take your choice or try them all; this a fine place to let your hair down.

When you're played out, follow the remains of the old cement slide downhill. This slide was a favorite of kids when the area was first opened. They waxed it with surfboard wax and slid down on pieces of carpet and burlap sacks, but after a number of concussions and broken arms, it was finally covered over.

Where the trail forks, go left. Look for caterpillar vine here; its leaves are fernlike and unremarkable, but in bloom, it resembles an invasion of green caterpillars.

Ahead are some coast prickly pear cacti, and farther on, a set of wooden steps. Take them up to a section of trail that's especially pretty in late winter and spring when the red paintbrush, purple nightshade, blue-eyed grass, and bright green mosses and ferns are all at their best.

At the clearing up ahead, you can see telegraph weed, the tall Hooker's evening primrose, and tree tobacco, a South American import too poisonous to smoke, but used by local Indians to treat rheumatism and swollen glands.

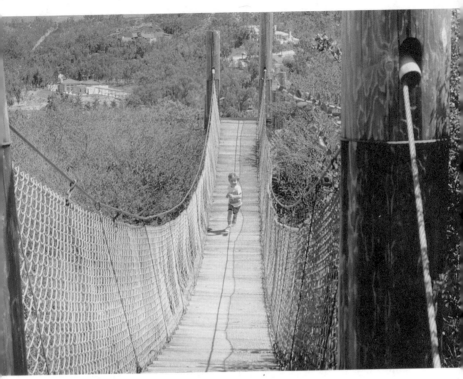

Swinging bridge at Activity Hill (Photo by Barbara Moore)

If you want, try the trail to your right. It's less interesting than the previous section, mostly just buckwheat, black sage, and broom, but it's a short walk and not unpleasant.

Broom, by the way, is often found in areas once cleared for farming. Seventy-five years ago, Solana Beach was covered with acres of lima beans, a crop that needed no irrigation, an important consideration in water-starved Southern California. Broom has taken over these lower, flatter places where beans once grew; higher, steeper locations are virtually broomless.

From the clearing, bear left to the service road, then take a left and go past the Scout Camp and Scout House, designed for tenderfoot campers whose outdoor experience may include a dip in the pool of the country club across the street. Now you're back in civilization again, with playgrounds, restrooms, a ballfield, and a group picnic area just ahead. The ranger office is here, and also an information kiosk. Up the hill to your right are more picnic and play areas, and the Upper Entrance. This is a good time to stop for lunch, or try a new activity.

A Word About Chaparral

Chaparral, the most common plant community in San Diego, is as typical of the area as pine forests are of the mountains. It takes its name from a Mexican word for scrub oak: *chaparro*, meaning "shorty." Nineteenth-century vaqueros—Mexican cowboys—invented the protective leg coverings called *chaps* when they grew tired of beating their way through the brambles while rounding up stray cattle. Originally, even their horses wore chaps.

Chaparral is often referred to as coastal sage scrub, although strictly speaking, chaparral is the taller, evergreen stuff, like lemonade berry and laurel sumac. Sage scrub tends to be shorter, more aromatic, and have softer leaves, like sagebrush. Some naturalists call the whole community an "elfin forest"—a pretty term for a group of short trees and bushes that are forest enough for the small animals living among them.

Chaparral plants are opportunistic, which means they take advantage of the slightest rainfall to bloom, drop their seeds, and carry on the species. They have to be tough to survive the long dry periods in Southern California. All year long, they hoard water in their small waxy leaves and deep roots. In summer, when there's almost no water to be had, most of them lie dormant, just as some animals hibernate to survive the winter. During this time, they can catch fire easily, and the flames spread . . . well, like wildfire. Afterwards, the land may look dead and bare, but the first drops of rain bring an amazing burst of new life.

Brush fires are actually good for the chaparral. Some plants inhibit the growth of others, and fire clears out areas so new plants can grow. It also gets rid of dead wood and gives certain seeds the conditions they need for sprouting. Some seeds may wait in the ground for years until a fire cracks their tough outer coatings enough to make them susceptible to the next rainfall. The early natives of San Diego knew this, and often set fire to an area they expected to return to later on, assuring themselves of a good harvest.

Chaparral plants have another interesting way of dealing with fire. Just weeks after a blaze has turned shrubs into charred skeletons, green shoots start springing up from the underground burls that escaped the heat of the flames. This kind of plant reincarnation is called crown sprouting.

One final word: If you come from a place of tall trees or green meadows, you may think chaparral is the kind of stuff only a botanist could love. You'll probably find it dry and disappointing at first, but the more you know about it, the more it will grow on you. Promise.

When you're ready to leave, take the dirt road from the upper parking lot and walk east. Bear right at the fork, and continue downhill, passing the small Wedding Pond, till you're back on the paved road again. Or, if you're still game, try any of the small trails branching off into the "bush."

Some of these paths are so overgrown, you'll feel as if you're out in the middle of nowhere. If you're lucky, you might see a family of California quail. If not, you'll have something to look forward to on your next visit.

3 TORREY PINES STATE RESERVE

LOCATION
Del Mar/La Jolla.

Main Reserve
From I-5, take the Carmel Valley Road exit and go west to the light at North Torrey Pines Road. Turn left, cross Peñasquitos Lagoon, and look for the entrance road 0.5 mile south on your right. Drive uphill and park near the Visitor's Lodge (TG1207:G2).

East Grove
Flintkote Avenue: From I-5, take Carmel Valley Road east to El Camino Real. Turn right and continue to Carmel Mountain Road. Turn right, then turn left onto Sorrento Valley Road. At the light at Sorrento Valley Boulevard, turn right, then right again onto Roselle. Stay on Roselle until it dead-ends on Estuary. Turn left, then turn right onto Flintkote. Park where you can (TG1208:A5).

Torrey Pines Extension
Del Mar Scenic Parkway: From I-5, take the Carmel Valley Road exit and go west to Del Mar Scenic Parkway, just opposite the North Beach parking lot. Turn right and continue on to the end of the street. Park near the tennis court (TG1207:H1).

Mira Montana: From I-5, take the Del Mar Heights Road exit and go west to Mercado. Turn left, then left again onto Cordero. Go two blocks; turn right on Mira Montana. Park in the small parking area (TG1187:H7).

HOURS
Main reserve and Visitor's Lodge, 8:00 A.M. to sunset. Day-use fee. East Grove and the Extension, sunrise to sunset; no fee.

Torrey Pines State Reserve

DESCRIPTION

"Torrey Pines State Reserve is a majestic wilderness island amidst an increasingly urban area," says the visitor's guide, and so it is. It includes about 2000 acres of spectacular cliffs, canyons, mesas, beaches, and wetlands spread out over three locations.

The 1000-acre main reserve has the greatest concentration of Torrey pines, more than 3000 of them. These rare trees are found in only one other location on Santa Rosa Island, off Santa Barbara.

At park headquarters in the Visitor's Lodge, there are interactive displays of some of the animals and birds that live in the reserve, and a small but interesting bookshop. A board outside the office gives information on what's in bloom. In front of the lodge is a labeled native plant garden where you can check your knowledge. Volunteers offer excellent slide shows and guided walks on weekends at 10:00 A.M. and 2:00 P.M. The park can get really crowded on weekend afternoons; try to come early, or during the week.

There are restrooms and drinking fountains across from the lodge's parking lot. Outside the main reserve, there are no facilities.

HISTORY

Centuries ago, Indians came here to gather seeds from the cones of the Torrey pines. Spanish explorers, noticing that this was the only tree-covered section of coastline in the area, named it Punta de los Arboles or "Tree Point." American navigators used it as a landmark, calling it Pine Hill.

In 1850, the year California became a state, Dr. C. C. Parry, official botanist for the U.S.–Mexican boundary survey, identified the Torrey pine as a new species. He named it after his friend, botanist John Torrey.

Unique and hardy, the Torrey pine gradually acquired staunch supporters among local conservationists. By 1885, it was a criminal offense to cut down any of the trees, which picnickers had been using for firewood.

In 1899, the city of San Diego established 369 acres as a public park. Philanthropist Ellen Browning Scripps began buying land to the north to add to the park, and in 1921 she appointed Guy Fleming custodian of the newly named Torrey Pines Reserve.

Fleming, a dedicated conservationist and park administrator, had worked on the planning and planting of Balboa Park. Later, as District Supervisor of State Parks, he oversaw the development of Anza-Borrego, Palomar Mountain, Cuyamaca, and Coronado's Silver Strand. The home he built on the reserve is used today as a ranger residence. In 1923, the Torrey Pines Lodge was opened as a restaurant and gift shop and became a regular tour bus lunch stop. It is now the park's headquarters and the site of its small museum.

Ownership of the reserve was transferred to the state of California in the 1950s. One hundred acres were set aside at the south end for construction of a public golf course. Continued public interest and support have added Torrey Pines Extension, Peñasquitos Lagoon, and other small parcels to the original park acreage.

MAIN RESERVE

The main reserve has a number of well-maintained trails that are beautiful all year long. All distances are round trip from the lodge, where trail maps are always available.

Needles and cones

Walk 1—High Point Trail

Distance: 0.7 mile round trip. *Time:* 15 minutes.

As its name implies, this is the highest point in the reserve, with a commanding view eastward across the lagoon to distant Black Mountain, and southwest to La Jolla and the ocean. Rangers call this the "100-yard walk," and the climb up to the High Point bench is just about that. The walk along the road from the lodge to the trailhead is longer than the trail itself; you'd do well to combine this with another trail.

Across from the trailhead is a large Torrey pine with an odd, dense clump of needles that looks like a huge nest. Actually, it's an abnormality called "witch's broom," which may be a virus, a genetic disorder, or a kind of tree wart. There are several more examples within the reserve, but this is the most noticeable.

Walk 2—Guy Fleming Trail

Distance: 1.3 miles round trip. *Time:* 45 minutes.

This was park supervisor Fleming's favorite walk, named in his honor after he died. To reach the trailhead, walk 0.25 mile down the road from the lodge, or park at the closer North Grove parking lot. A spring wildflower calendar/map, available for 25 cents at the lodge's bookshop, is nice to have in hand, especially from February to July, when most plants are blooming.

We like to start out by going due west, where the trail winds around a canyon wall. Two ocean overlooks provide good vantage points for watching playful dolphins and, in winter, the southward migration of California gray whales. Sometimes you can spot "rafts" of sleeping sea lions, their flippers held out of the water to catch the warmth of the sun.

Notice how the trees in this area are bent nearly to the ground, beaten down by the constant wind and salt air. After the crest of the hill, the trees stand tall and upright again, because they're more protected.

Just before the end of the trail is a birdbath, with a bench across the way. If you sit quietly for awhile, you may see a fox or a deer coming around for a drink, or more often, a scrub jay or a finch dropping in for a dip.

Walk 3—The Parry Grove Trail
Distance: 0.75 mile round trip. *Time:* 20 to 30 minutes.

Named for the botanist who named the Torrey pines, this trail used to be the shadiest in the reserve until an infestation of bark beetle killed most of the trees in the early 1990s. Since then, new trees have sprouted, and there are still wonderful ocean views.

Just across from High Point, you can visit a labeled native plant garden, which introduces you to some of the plants you'll see along the way. In spring, near the back-to-back benches, look for low-growing scarlet pimpernel. Really a coral color, these tiny flowers are called the "poor man's weatherglass" because they close up when the weather turns cloudy.

To your right, just past the benches, is a hedge of Cleveland sage, which has the nicest scent and the prettiest blue flowers of all the sages. Once it grew wild over the hills of Del Mar; now, with so much land covered with housing, it's almost disappeared.

Walk 4—Beach Trail/Razor Point Trail Circuit
Distance: 2 miles round trip. *Time:* 1 to 1.5 hours.

Our very favorite hike in the reserve is really a combination of trails. Start out just north of the restrooms, following the sign to the Beach Trail, a mile-long route that's popular with local runners.

As you walk (or run) along, notice how the chaparral shrubs look as neat as if a gardener had trimmed them; this, too, is caused by the wind and salt air that mow down the plants on exposed slopes. The next part of the trail is especially pretty in spring, when there are often more than 50 different kinds of wildflowers in bloom on a single day.

Just before the second bench on the trail, you'll reach a junction. The steps just ahead lead down about 0.25 mile past spectacular views of cliffs and sea to Torrey Pines State Beach. Getting onto the sand involves

Torrey Pines State Reserve

negotiating a few yards of narrow cliff-side trail near the end, so watch your step. From here, you can walk south to Black's Beach, admiring the cliffs from below. If you don't feel sure-footed enough to go all the way down, you can still enjoy the view before heading back to the bench junction.

With or without the beach interlude, go west from the junction to the Yucca Point sign. Follow it left to the overlook, where you'll see one of the largest concentrations of Mojave yucca in the reserve, plus a few narrow-leafed Whipple's yuccas. Look for the giant asparagus stalks in early spring, followed by white flower clusters and, finally, pickle-shaped seed pods.

Returning to the main trail, take the first left and head north past Big Basin, a wide bowl bordered by red badlands cliffs carved by eons of storm runoff. Stop on the small wooden bridge and look down into the narrow canyon where, in spring, there are patches of bright green ferns clinging to the pale yellow sandstone. Ahead, the trail forks left to the Razor Point overlooks, and more dramatic views of the coast.

Keeping to the main trail, you'll soon reach the first of several fenced overlooks into the Canyon of the Swifts. You might see a swift or two in spring or summer. If so, watch carefully; they have the unique habit of mating on the wing.

The dead trees you may see along the trail are the result of a recent infestation of hungry beetles that drill their way through to the inner bark and often prove fatal to drought-weakened trees. Farther along are the only native orchids we know of in the coastal area, a few stalks of tiny green flowers. They're no match for Hawaiian orchids, but it's amazing they can grow here at all.

At the next overlook, scan the canyon's small caves for great horned owls, ravens, and swifts, all of which like to nest here in spring. This part of the canyon is split by the Carmel Valley earthquake fault, a branch of the Rose Canyon fault system that runs along I-5, up Ardath Road, and out past the La Jolla Beach and Tennis Club. Longtime residents remember the old trail at the canyon's bottom, so narrow it was called Fat Man's Misery.

The path winds away and then back along the canyon, climbing steadily. (If looking down bothers you, there's a small trail to the right just before the third overlook that leads up over Red Butte, connecting with the main trail once the canyon's safely behind you.) At the top of the steps bear left; the right-hand trail leads up to Red Butte. Soon you'll come to the first part of the beach trail. Go left, and it won't be long until you're back at the restrooms across from the lodge.

EAST GROVE

Walk 5

Distance: 6 miles round trip to beach. *Time:* 2 to 2.5 hours.

This is a good, get-away-from-it-all trail. You will hear the distant sound of traffic, and occasionally, a train will pass close enough to let you wave to the engineer, but you'll probably have the place to yourself. After heavy rain or if Peñasquitos Lagoon is full, your walk here will be a lot shorter; the trail could flood out after the first half mile or so.

From the gate, follow the rutted road for just over a mile, passing the ranger's residence about halfway. Where the road bears right, follow the path toward the cliffs through the sagebrush, fennel, and telegraph weed. In spring, among the wildflowers, look for orange fiddleneck, which kids used to whisper would make you wet your bed at night if you touched it. To your left, above the chaparral, you'll see a few Torrey pines. There were more until 1972, when an angry young man disappointed in love set the grove on fire. Subsequent planting of ryegrass for erosion control actually inhibited the regrowth of native plants and trees.

The tall pale bluffs, pockmarked by eons of erosion, are part of the Torrey sandstone whose formation began forty million years ago. Today, owls and ravens like to nest in the small cavelike hollows.

After half a mile, the trail dips down and the vegetation changes; you'll see water-loving plants like alkali heath, pickleweed, and salt grass. When the lagoon is full, this may be as far as you can go. As you round the point across from the railroad trestle, notice the white "icing" in the dried mud. If you were to taste it (yuck!) you'd know what it is in a second—salt. This is a salt marsh, and all the plants here have to be able to tolerate a lot of salt in their soil.

Look up on the hillside to your left; the bits of white shell sticking out are the remains of ancient La Jollan Indian kitchen middens, or trash heaps. Pay attention to the tall clumps of round reed; those long, pointed quills can tattoo your legs if you're not careful.

We call this the "animal track trail" because deer, coyote, and raccoon tracks can almost always be found here. Animals come here daily to drink from Peñasquitos Creek, and even if you never get to see them, you can learn a lot from studying their tracks. Coyotes, for example, walk a straight line, one paw in front of the other, unlike dogs or other animals. Deer step with their hind feet almost in the same spot as their front feet. Raccoon tracks look like the handprints of human babies.

In drier months, you can follow this trail through the pickleweed all the way to the beach, crossing busy North Torrey Pines Road. Your energy and the lagoon's water level will determine the turnaround point.

TORREY PINES EXTENSION

In the late 1960s, the Extension was well on its way to becoming another condominium complex. Developers had already cleared a road through the valley, cut down several trees, and installed a storm drain before a determined citizen's group raised enough money to save the land. Despite some permanent damage, primarily the turning of a seasonal stream into a deep erosion gully, the Extension is today a quiet and lovely place to walk, even after rain.

A wide valley separates two distinctly different upland areas. The eastern section, Trail A, is drier and has few trees, while the western ridge, Trail B and the D.A.R. trail system, offers pine-shaded ocean views. We like to connect the trails in a figure-eight loop.

Walk 6—Margaret Fleming Trail A
Distance: 0.75 mile round trip. *Time:* 45 minutes.

Just after you enter the Extension, two signs mark trails named for Guy Fleming's wife. Born Margaret Doubleday Eddy, she was a wealthy New Jersey debutante, the niece of Abner Doubleday, who invented modern baseball. On a visit to La Jolla, she fell in love with Fleming, and soon gave up East Coast society for San Diego's great outdoors. Her nature etchings and lithographs were widely exhibited, and she was one of the major forces in the Extension's acquisition.

Trail A begins at the right fork, gradually climbing through black sage, sagebrush, and bush sunflower. The lone Torrey pine you see just after the wooden steps shows the black scars of a fire that swept through here in 1962. Numbered markers are the remains of an old nature trail for which guides are available at park headquarters.

At #18, near a "tunnel" of laurel sumac, is an old wood rat's nest; it's on the right, and looks like a large pile of dry, brown sticks. Wood rats, sometimes called pack rats, are nocturnal animals that build elaborate nests with separate bedrooms, bathrooms, pantries, and nurseries. There are a number of these nests in the Extension, some of them hundreds of years old.

Farther along on your right, look for the bright yellow blossoms of tree poppy among the shorter bush sunflowers. Tree poppy usually grows in disturbed areas, especially after fires. After you pass through another "tunnel" of ceanothus (#16), there's some bee plant, whose large toothed leaves and tiny red blossoms are noticeable in spring. Despite its name, we've never seen any bees hovering around it.

Look for toyon, whose red berries start appearing in late fall, and spice bush, our native citrus, near #14. Some people are allergic to its oil, which can make the skin hypersensitive to sun. The fruits look like tiny oranges.

A bit farther on is yerba santa, the "holy herb," whose pale fuzzy leaves are sometimes called "nature's bandaids." In spring, clusters of lavender flowers improve its odd, ungainly appearance.

A set of wooden stairs will take you past a dense stand of scrub oak (#11) and onto a sandstone ridge that leads to a chamise-covered mesa.

Keeping the red rock outcroppings on your right, head north on the path through the shrubs. In early spring, you'll see and smell a field of wild onions. Toward May, the area is pink with low-growing canchalagua, whose bright star-shaped flowers like the dry hard soil here.

Where the trail forks up ahead, go left, unless you want to check out the Red Ridge Trail (Walk 8) and add another half hour to your outing. Walk down more steps, passing clumps of yellow rockrose in spring, and showy scarlet larkspur in June. Hummingbirds love the larkspur, and this is one of the few places in the county where it can be found. After the steps, you'll cross over the roots of a large Torrey pine, the one about 20 feet to your left. The Torrey pine's root system can extend out hundreds of feet in its search for water.

The next section of trail once involved scrambling into and out of a gully. It's been civilized by the addition of two wooden bridges and leads through tall ryegrass to the Extension's main trail. If you go left, you head back to the entrance. We usually like to go right, and take the path curving left and uphill to the D.A.R. Trail and Trail B.

Walk 7—Margaret Fleming Trail B and the D.A.R. Trail System

Distance: Up to 2 miles round trip. *Time:* 45 minutes to 1 hour.

If you start from the Extension trailhead, go past Trail A and pick up Trail B farther on. Take the first left up a series of wooden steps that lead to the western ridge and the D.A.R. trail system, funded by the California Daughters of the American Revolution. Along this path, you'll pass white sage, wild cucumber, Mojave yuccas, and, in early spring, yellow sea dahlias. At the top of the ridge, there's a panoramic view of the ocean.

Here you have three choices:

You can go left along the ridge to a cul-de-sac that overlooks the lagoon, the main reserve, and the ocean. This is a great place to be at sunset; there's even a bench to sit on.

Or, you can follow the fence to your right, heading down some steps and into a tree-lined trail with the piney smell of the Sierras. Look for purple snapdragon and red Indian pinks here in spring. There's another bench just before you cross the wooden bridge and go left, down a steep flight of steps into a small canyon.

The third option is continue up and along the main D.A.R. trail, taking the sharp right that leads away from the ridge-top fence. While you admire the view, keep an eye out for coast horned lizards, those endangered miniature dinosaurs that tend to blend in with their surroundings and are generally sand-colored here. We used to see them often; you'll be lucky to see one these days.

The trail rises slightly, then goes down more steps past summer-blooming sand aster, lavender flowers with yellow centers. Passing toyon and yerba santa, you'll soon come to a junction. Straight up the hill is Mar Scenic Drive, an alternative entrance to the Extension. Downhill to the right is the trail to follow if you want to go out the way you came in. (When we go from Trail A to Trail B, this is where we connect.) Note the rock-filled wire cages in the gully; they're gabions, designed to slow erosion, but not terribly effective. If not for conservationists, this would have been part of Del Mar Scenic Parkway.

Walk 8—Mira Montana Entrance: The Red Ridge Trail

Distance: 1 mile round trip. *Time:* 30 minutes.

This flat, sandy trail is popular with local runners and walkers. From the parking area, go south a few hundred yards to the metal gate. Inside, on the left, are several large clumps of fragrant Cleveland sage.

Where the trail divides around a stand of Torrey pines, look for biscuit root, a member of the carrot family, whose pale yellow spring flowers turn to maroon seed-pod clusters that dry to beige in early summer. Though considered inedible, it got its name from explorers Lewis and Clark, who ate the roots of a similar plant and thought it tasted like stale biscuits.

As you walk on, you'll get a bird's-eye view of the incredible spread of development to the east. To the west is the more restful sight of the sea.

From May to July, if you think you smell a skunk, look for skunkweed, a ground-hugging thistle-like plant with small lavender flowers. Nearby you should also see pink Turkish rugging and green mats of tread lightly, two other short, prickly plants.

Take the trail to its southern end, a red ridge overlooking a rugged canyon, then circle back along the eastern rim.

4 LOS PEÑASQUITOS CANYON PRESERVE

LOCATION
Sorrento Valley/Mira Mesa.

West End—Sorrento Valley: From North County, take I-5 to Carmel Valley Road, then go east to El Camino Real. Turn right and continue to Carmel Mountain Road; turn right. At Sorrento Valley Road, turn left and continue to Sorrento Valley Boulevard. Turn left again at the light and go 1 mile to the staging area on the right. From San Diego, take I-805 to Sorrento Valley Road. Turn right on Mira Mesa Boulevard (which becomes Sorrento Valley Road) and continue to Sorrento Valley Boulevard. Turn right at the light and continue to the staging area on the right (TG1208:D5).

Lopez Canyon—Sorrento Mesa: Take I-805 north to Mira Mesa Boulevard. Go east to Pacific Heights Boulevard; turn left. At the next light, Pacific Mesa Boulevard, turn right. Go to the end and park (TG1208:F5).

East End—Peñasquitos/Mira Mesa: Take I-15 north to Mercy Road. Go west to Black Mountain Road and the entrance of the park. Parking fee. (TG1189:D7).

HOURS
8:00 A.M. to sunset.

DESCRIPTION
A good choice for long and short hikes is Los Peñasquitos Canyon Preserve, with its meadows, tree-lined trails, and wide-open spaces. This 4100-acre natural park, jointly owned by city and county, was invaded in early 1988 by developers who built a 20-foot-high vehicle road from the west entrance to Lopez Ridge. It's still a fine place to walk, though, and popular with mountain bikers and horseback riders too. There are creeks to cross, shallow pools to cool your feet in, even a little waterfall. Seven miles long from end to end, the canyon is a haven for wildlife. There are portapotties at each end. For information and guided walks, call (858) 484-3219.

HISTORY
The canyon called Los Peñasquitos, "The Little Cliffs," was the first private land grant in San Diego County. In 1823, ten years before the missions were secularized and their properties divided, 8000 acres of good grazing land were given to Presidio Commander Francisco Maria Ruiz. At seventy-six, Ruiz, who built the first house in Old Town, built the first house outside it, near the east end of the canyon. Unmarried, he moved in with the family of his grandnephew Francisco Maria Alvarado, who looked after him until his death ten years later. Before he died, he transferred the entire property to Alvarado.

In 1846, the rancho was the first rest stop for General Kearny's battered Army of the West after the Battle of San Pasqual. Knowing Alvarado's anti-American sympathies, Kearny's men raided his land for cattle, food, and supplies. Alvarado's daughter ended up marrying an American, Colorado River boat captain George Alonzo Johnson. The ranch house they lived in is now a historic site.

In the 1880s, Jacob Shell Taylor, developer of old Del Mar, bought the rancho and converted the house into a hotel. Afterwards, cattle interests took over the property, and the original buildings were used as bunkhouses for ranch hands.

The county acquired the 200 acres around the Johnson-Taylor Adobe in 1974, and the lion's share of the property was purchased by the city a few years later. It was established as a preserve in 1980.

WEST END

Before the construction of Calle Cristobal and the development of Lopez Ridge, this area was one of our favorites. Cattle grazed here for 150 years, until 1989. We don't miss the cow pies, but we do miss the cows—they gave us a real sense of rancho history.

Today, the trail heading left under the bridge and uphill is a good place for a glimpse of the ruined adobe, "El Cuervo," built by Alvarado's son Diego, and the old corral that was used for inoculating cattle. Walk downhill to meet up with Walk 1.

Walk 1—The Road to Yuma
Distance: 6 miles round trip. *Time:* 3 to 3.5 hours.

One hundred and fifty years ago, wagons loaded with supplies traveled this road from San Diego to army posts at Yuma. Now it's the most popular trail in the canyon, enjoyed by joggers, horseback riders, mountain bikers, birders, and ordinary strollers all year long.

Heading east, after the first rise, about 1.5 miles in, you'll see some of the palisades of volcanic rock that give Peñasquitos its name. Look over the side to see chaparral ferns and red-flowered dudleya hugging the north-facing rocks. About 3 miles in from the entrance is the waterfall. It's no Niagara, and only a trickle in summer, but it's always a nice place to relax. If you're feeling ambitious, continue on to Black Mountain Road, another 3 miles ahead.

Walk 2—Meadow to Waterfall Trail
Distance: 6 miles round trip. *Time:* 3 to 3.5 hours.

Take the main trail to the creek crossing near the 1-mile marker to pick up one of the flattest, least traveled, and prettiest trails in the canyon. You'll probably have to get your feet wet, but we think it's worth it.

On the north side of the creek, follow the cowpath across the meadow. Along the creek bed are trees typical of the streamside community: willows, sycamores, elderberries, and one of the few coast live oaks in this end of the canyon. In winter and early spring, when the sycamores are still bare, you can see the large stick nests of hawks and owls; each year a different pair of birds appropriates a nest. If you're tempted to stretch out at the

Peñasquitos Canyon, West End

foot of one of the trees, think again; there's lots of poison oak twining around the trunks.

The south-facing slopes you pass are drier than the north-facing ones because they're not as protected from the sun. Some of them are covered with brownish green jojoba, an ingredient in shampoos and cosmetics. Because it produces a very fine oil, local conservationists tried to grow it commercially a few years back, but jojoba needs more care than they expected, and they soon gave up.

In May, near the creek, hedges of wild roses start blooming. They smell wonderful and look just like old-fashioned pink tea roses.

At about 1.5 miles, you'll come to more peñasquitos. This green-colored rock is part of a volcanic island chain formed underwater 140 million years ago. Standing on the ridge, you can see in the distance the rock outcropping where the waterfall is, about another 1.5 miles ahead. Just before the waterfall are two concrete bridges. After crossing, you can head down to the water, cross over the rocks, have a little R and R, and take the main trail back. Or you can continue on about a mile to Carson's Crossing, named for frontier scout Kit Carson, who fought in the Battle of San Pasqual, a brief comedy of errors that ended in American defeat.

After the battle, Carson and two other volunteers made their way past mounted California sentries, crawling part of the way, to get help from San Diego for Kearny's exhausted troops, reduced to eating their mounts at Mule Hill, near what is now Rancho Bernardo. He may well have crossed here; you can take off your shoes for the same short wade and then follow the main road back to Sorrento Valley, or continue east to Black Mountain Road.

LOPEZ CANYON

In the 1840s, this canyon area was given as a land grant to Bonifacio Lopez, a master horseman who liked to take the hills at a gallop, despite his weight of 300 pounds. His descendants lived in the house he built for more than 100 years.

From the "Lopez Canyon" sign on Sorrento Mesa, there's a nice view eastward across the canyon to Black Mountain, with the ever-developing community of Peñasquitos climbing up its base. To the south is Mount Woodson, with Mira Mesa in the foreground. Directly across the canyon is the Wildlife Corridor, a tunnel installed by developers to provide a passage between Peñasquitos and Lopez Canyons.

In spring, the south-facing hillsides are covered with yellow mustard, which in wet years can grow up to 6 feet tall. A cabbage relative, mustard can bloom from late winter to midsummer. Legend has it that mustard was introduced by the padres, who scattered seeds so the flowers would mark their trail as they traveled from mission to mission. The seeds are used to make the yellow spread we put on our hot dogs.

You can also walk into Lopez Canyon from the west end of Peñasquitos (see West End directions above), a flatter and prettier approach.

Walk 3—Lopez Road
Distance: 3.5 miles round trip. *Time:* 2 hours.

To enter the canyon, take the old Lopez Road down to the rancho. You'll pass fennel, elderberry, horehound, fuchsia-flowered gooseberry, wild cucumber, and, in spring, fields of buttercups. Descending, you'll leave behind the roar of jets from nearby Miramar Air Station and the whirring of model planes sent off from the mesa top by local enthusiasts and start to hear the chirping of crickets, the creaking of tree frogs, and the trill of meadowlarks.

At the bottom, where the road forks, go right. Here are sycamores, with clumps of mistletoe hanging from their branches. Mistletoe berries are a favorite food of many birds that help spread this parasite by leaving behind droppings full of seeds. In spring, hawks and owls like to nest in the sycamores; keep an eye out for their large stick nests, and you might see a parent bird feeding its young or pushing a fledgling off a branch to teach it to hunt.

Head east along Lopez Creek, a pleasantly babbling brook in winter, a dry, cobbled streambed in summer. The jeep road you're following crisscrosses the creek, impassable after heavy rains. In spring, look for tadpoles in the still ponds; in summer, they turn into the tiny green tree frogs sometimes called "Hollywood frogs" because they can be heard on the soundtracks of so many films and TV shows shot on location in Southern California.

The road becomes more and more cobbly, and, after the pepper trees, drier and less interesting, but you can walk on for another 3 miles and have a better chance of seeing deer, coyotes, or rattlers than another human. The trail comes to an end at Montongo Street in Mira Mesa.

EAST END

The entrance here was specially designed for horse trailers; ordinary cars are asked to park in the upper paved area. The main trail, a maintenance road now used by the water department, follows the old stage road to Yuma. All walks start at the gate just past the information kiosk north of the caretaker's mobile home.

On the north side of Peñasquitos Creek, invisible from here, is Canyonside Park, with its tennis courts, ballfields, and restrooms. A surge of recent development has made the area a lot less rural than it used to be, but the East End's charms will soon make you forget the suburban invasion.

After winter rains, the road may be muddy, but that's the best time to look for tracks of deer, coyote, raccoons, and, of course, horses. There are stables across the street at Horseman's Park, where you can rent horses for trail rides.

Walk 4—Adobe Trail

Distance: 2 miles round trip. *Time:* 1 hour.

Go west along the main road to the Ranch House Crossing. To avoid getting your feet wet, go a bit west of the vehicle crossing to the wooden bridge. Once across, go north a few feet to rejoin the dirt crossroad. Take the first clearly defined path to the left, which leads past the overflow parking lot to an open area and the old ranch house and barn.

The historic adobe, covered with plaster and wood, now houses the ranger office, where tours are scheduled on Saturdays at 11:00 A.M.

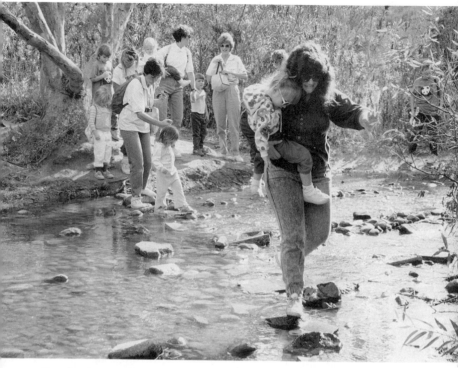

Crossing Peñasquitos Creek, East End (Photo by Barbara Moore)

On the creek side of the adobe are several huge pepper and palm trees that could be as old as the house itself. Down by the creek are an old stone springhouse, used to store perishables in pre-refrigerator days, a wooden shed, and a leaky stone cistern with a new roof. Owls like to roost in the trees here; look for their fur-ball pellets on the ground.

Just past the cistern are the remains of an old fence. Stay close to the willows, and you'll see a path leading down to a board crossing of a narrow part of the creek. For a more adventurous return, follow the narrow path past the burbling creek, through a grassy clearing. Just ahead, you'll have to cross a short stretch that can get pretty muddy in winter. Step lively here and you won't sink in up to your shoelaces. Continue on the path till you get to the creek crossing—you can always get the mud off your shoes there.

Alternatively, go back exactly the way you came. Either way, you'll cross the creek, pick up the vehicle road again, and bear left on the main road near sewer standpipe #86. The entrance is about 0.5 mile away. If you want to walk on, turn right at the main road, and pick up Walk 5.

Walk 5—Woodland to Waterfall Trail
Distance: 9 miles round trip. *Time:* 3.5 to 4 hours.

This is our favorite walk in the canyon, a beautifully wooded trail with a secluded feeling, quite different from the open-range country of the West End. Here you'll get a real sense of streamside San Diego, a leafy oasis of small groves and meadows in the midst of the dry chaparral. Those 9 miles may sound long, but they are lovely, and you can stop at any of the groves along the way if you don't want to go the whole distance.

Take the main road from the gate, passing the first crossroad and continuing west. At the next fork, you can bear left to a fallen live oak tree, one of the largest in the preserve. It died of root rot, caused by runoff from the houses above. Nearby is the grave of John Eichar, a cook on the ranch here a century ago. Evidently, he's still remembered; we've seen bouquets of flowers left on his grave.

You can sit on the dead live oak amid the fennel, horehound, and elderberry, and meditate on the cycle of life and death in the canyon. Just keep out of the poison oak.

On the road again—any one will do, but we usually choose the one closest to the creek—the next long stretch is shaded by eucalyptus, sycamores, live oaks, palms, willows, and mulefat. Look for flashy black-and-white acorn woodpeckers that use the dead snags of sycamores as acorn pantries. An entire woodpecker family will maintain a storage tree for years, sometimes making as many as 20,000 holes in one tree. In late fall and winter, keep an eye out for red-eyed phainopeplas, foraging among the red berries of toyon—the California holly.

A narrow trail forks off to the right, winding in and out of the trees. This is a pretty section of trail and follows the creek until it rejoins the main road at about 2 miles.

At 2.5 miles, you reach Carson's Crossing. You can dip your feet in the creek here, or stop for a picnic. We usually press on to the waterfall, continuing ever westward, bearing right at the fork under the powerlines.

At about 3 miles, you'll see a rock outcropping at the top of the rise ahead. That's where the waterfall is, and you're almost there. Go right here and follow the path down to the edge of the gorge to rest or picnic on the peñasquitos.

When you're ready to leave, take the main road back. It's not as secluded, but it will cut about a mile off your round-trip distance.

If you're lucky, as we've been on several occasions, you might see one of the canyon's resident bobcats walking across the road. They look like long-legged housecats, but won't respond to a call of "Here, kitty, kitty." There's an equally good chance of spotting a deer or coyote. Peñasquitos is the last refuge of local wildlife.

⑤ BLACK'S CANYON AND SCRIPPS COASTAL RESERVE

LOCATION
La Jolla.

Black's Canyon: Take I-5 to La Jolla Village Drive, go west past the University of California (UCSD) campus to La Jolla Shores Drive; take a left and a quick right to La Jolla Farms Road. The entrance gate is on your left, about 0.5 mile in, opposite Black Gold Road. Unless you're planning a short stay, park at the end of the two-hour parking signs a few hundred yards ahead, and walk back to the gate (TG1227:J1).

Scripps Coastal Reserve: Heading back toward La Jolla Shores on La Jolla Farms Road, look on the right for a circular drive and a tall wooden fence with a black metal gate. The sign says "Scripps Coastal Reserve." Park where you can (TG1227:J2).

HOURS
Sunrise to sunset.

DESCRIPTION
At Black's Canyon, a dramatic descent from the million-dollar mesa-top homes of La Jolla Farms leads to one of the county's best and least accessible beaches. Wonderful ocean views framed by steep green slopes greet you at every switchback of this paved vehicle road, which is closed to all cars but those of local residents lucky enough to have access keys. Strong-legged bicyclers, joggers, and board-toting surfers frequent this route,

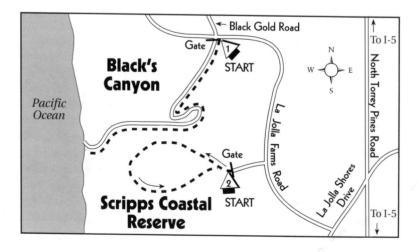

which is the safest shortcut to celebrated Black's Beach. The southern section of beach is owned by UCSD; the city-owned section extends up to state-owned Torrey Pines Beach.

Just down the street is Scripps Coastal Reserve, an archaeological site that is part of the University of California's Natural Reserve System, which protects sensitive habitats and endangered plants and animals. There are equally wonderful views here, but no beach access.

Aside from a pay phone at the top of Black's Canyon, there are no facilities.

HISTORY

The La Jolla Farms area was developed in the late 1940s by William H. Black, a Texas oil millionaire, who bought up 200 acres of the Biological Cliffs Hunting Reserve owned by the Scripps family and located between World War II Camp Callan and the ocean.

View from the top of Scripps Coastal Reserve

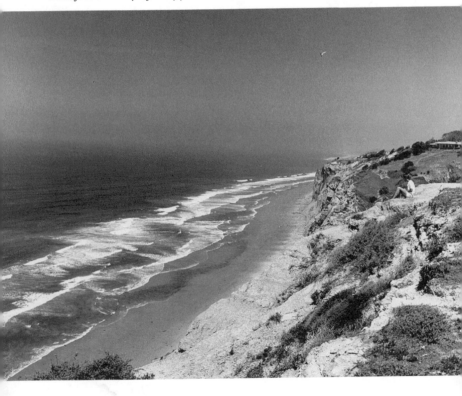

Originally, he was going to reserve the land for a few select friends who could afford fine homes and horses. He built Blackgold Stables on Torrey Pines Road to train thoroughbred racehorses and polo ponies; riding trails led from the stables down to the beach.

Ultimately, Black subdivided his property into 1- and 2-acre sites including stable use and membership in his Bridle Club. In 1967, he died on the golf course at the La Jolla Beach and Tennis Club, and UCSD acquired the still-unsold 130 acres from his son.

Black's Beach became a popular gathering place for nude sunbathers, and in 1974 the city of San Diego declared it a "swimsuit optional zone." By 1977, they had changed their minds, and the controversial legal status was revoked. For awhile, police issued tickets to underdressed beachgoers, who began to signal each other with whistles whenever the law was in sight.

Today, a truce prevails, though the Black family, embarrassed by all the to-do, has had its name officially removed from the beach.

BLACK'S CANYON

The Walk
Distance: 1.6 miles round trip. *Time:* 30 to 40 minutes.

This beautiful walk has an almost Hawaiian feel to it—if Hawaii had chaparral. On the slopes, you'll see sagebrush, lemonade berry, locoweed, prickly pear, cholla, and barrel cactus. The ravines, recipients of runoff from the homes above, are filled with the New Zealand import, myoporum, a fast-growing evergreen that loves salt air. In spring, look for orange-colored dodder covering the sage and the buckwheat. Picturesquely called devil's sewing thread or witch's hair, this leafless parasite was used by Indians as a cure for black widow spider bites; only the dodder on buckwheat was considered effective. There are signs of funnel spider nearby—their webs have a noticeable funnel at the center. Hidden at the base of its funnel, the spider waits for dinner to drop in.

In early spring, with the blooming of bush sunflower and sea dahlia, the hills are carpeted with yellow flowers. That's when you'll see wild cucumber, radish, and, if you're looking hard, some miner's lettuce and polypody ferns.

But the best feature of this walk, in any season, is its striking vistas of hillsides and sea. About halfway down, you'll start to hear the ocean's roar; till then, only birdsong breaks the silence. Look up now and again to catch a hawk making lazy circles in the sky, or a big black raven.

Down at the bottom, there's a pileup of rocks from recent slides; you may have to pick your way over some of them. It's never a good idea to stay too close to the crumbling sandstone cliffs, but they are impressive, 350 feet high and stretching up the coast all the way to Del Mar.

Once at the beach, you have three choices: go north, go south, or go home. If you're planning a beach walk, check a tidetable before you go; high tides can make parts of the trip impassable.

North along the beach is where the waves are best, the sandstone formations most varied, and where the beach turns "swimsuit optional." You may pass joggers wearing only their running shoes, a nude family frolicking with their dog, or, as we once did, a naked bagpiper playing "The Yellow Rose of Texas."

After about a mile, you may see a number of tiny people in the distance making their way down the cliffs from the Torrey Pines gliderport. This narrow, precipitous path is recommended only for the very hardy and sure of foot. The figures on the cliff top look remarkably antlike from here—and they're probably saying the same about you.

When the winds are right, there are hang gliders soaring overhead, one of the added attractions of Black's Beach. Glider planes used to take off from here too, but now they're only allowed on special occasions.

At low tide, you can usually walk all the way to the mouth of the San Dieguito River at the north end of Del Mar, a good 6 miles away. The green patch you see at about 2 miles is the Torrey Pines Golf Course. Just north of it is Torrey Pines State Reserve (see Chapter 3), where the cliff colors change from beige sandstone to the green, yellow, and red layers that indicate three different eras and are called, respectively, Delmar, Torrey, and Lindavista formations. The gray-green Delmar Formation is the lowest and oldest, and contains the fossil remains of oysters, clams, and other shellfish that lived in the seas 50 million years ago.

This long stretch of beach is great for picnics, but take your trash with you when you leave. In recent years, litter has been a problem here. There are only a few trash cans, often filled to overflowing, and garbage collection is sporadic.

If you choose to head **south along the beach**, you'll pass the "mushroom house," a beach house with its own private funicular (cable car) to the mesa top. The Coastal Commission would never allow this kind of construction now, but they've let it stand. It's about 0.5 mile to Dike Rock, one of the few volcanic formations on the coast; at low tide there are tidepools to explore.

Crossing under the Scripps Pier, you can continue south along La Jolla Shores Beach, for about another mile, stopping off for a drink or a snack on Avenida de la Playa.

Whatever you do, remember to save yourself for the trip back. It's a steep walk up from the beach, so take it easy.

SCRIPPS COASTAL RESERVE

The Walk

Distance: 0.7 mile loop. *Time:* 20 minutes.

Just off La Jolla Farms, overlooking the sea, is this ancient site inhabited by La Jollans 2000 to 5000 years ago.

Duck under the metal gate and follow the path through what was once an Indian village. Skeletal remains recovered from a dig here were stored in a garage for safekeeping during World War II, but somehow, by the end of the war, they had disappeared. One hopes they found a safe resting-place and weren't tossed out with the trash.

As you stroll past wild oats, foxtails, and other grasses, watch the sandy path for snake tracks and gopher holes. You'll see a lot of wild radish here in spring, its pastel flowers followed by seed pods that look like small green beans.

In the early part of the century, this was prime lima bean farmland. During World War II, foxholes and gun emplacements were set up to defend San Diego from attack by Japanese submarines.

The mound to your left as you head toward the water is all that's left of an old World War II rifle range. There were two military camps nearby: Camp Matthews, located where UCSD is today, and Camp Callan, near the present Torrey Pines Golf Course. No subs were ever sighted, but our boys were prepared.

Looking toward La Jolla

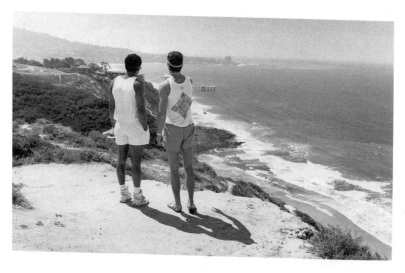

6 KATE SESSIONS MEMORIAL PARK

LOCATION
Pacific Beach. Take I-5 to the Garnet/Balboa exit. Go west to Lamont Street, which becomes Soledad Road. Turn right and continue past Loring, turning right at Park Drive, which leads to the parking area (TG1248:A4).

HOURS
Sunrise to sunset.

DESCRIPTION
Beautifully located on a hillside with panoramic views over Mission Bay, this 79-acre city park is really two parks in one: grassy slopes for picnicking, kite-flying, ball-playing, frisbee-tossing, and sunset-watching, and a section of scrub-covered open space for hiking. The developed area has picnic tables, barbecues, restrooms, and drinking water, as well as a 0.75-mile paved walking path. Many of the trees, benches, and drinking fountains have plaques commemorating donors. There's also a playground on the west side of the park, near the trailhead.

HISTORY
Kate Sessions was an eccentric ex-schoolteacher who started off working in a flower shop and ended up as San Diego's chief gardener. Known as the Mother of Balboa Park, she was responsible for convincing city fathers to give the old municipal park a new look. By the time of the 1915 Panama-California Exposition, she had helped fill it with hundreds of exotic trees and shrubs, a perfect complement to the romantic Spanish-Moorish architecture of the "temporary" exhibition buildings.

Not only Balboa Park, but all of San Diego benefited from Miss Sessions's beautiful tropical and subtropical plantings. In 1933, after her urging, the city set aside the area on Soledad Road for a park. Originally called Soledad Terrace Park, it was renamed for her in 1957, on the 100th anniversary of her birth. Not far away, at the corner of Garnet and Pico, where her last nursery was located, are a large Brazilian tipuana tree she planted and a plaque in her memory.

The Walk
Distance: 2 miles round trip. *Time:* 1 hour.

Start between the playground and the drinking fountain, at the park's northwest end, where, in summer, the gold-flowered tipuana trees are in full

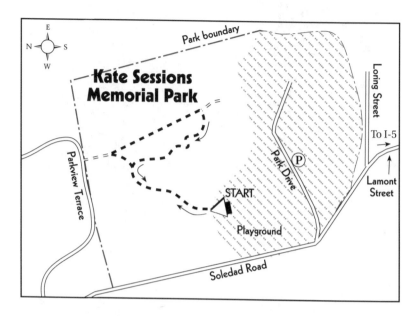

bloom. Follow the rough, often eroded trail through tall sage and taller lemonade berry. In spring, the hillsides are dotted with flowers, among them lavender bush mallow, a hollyhock relative. Look for patches of bedstraw, which grows in soft, thick mats and was used by Indians and early settlers to stuff mattresses, pillows, and chair cushions. An Old World variety was said to have lined the manger of the baby Jesus.

The trail leads down to the bottom of a small canyon where a creek sometimes runs in winter; it's usually dried up by the time the flowers appear. There are trapdoor spiders here, living behind ten-year-old doors, and huge black-and-gold bumblebees that love the blue-flowered black sage. You'll also see filaree, planted for sheep and cattle to graze on, and tumbleweed, a fall bloomer.

In spring, the wild cucumber shows its spiny green fruit, and the deerweed is covered with tiny yellow blossoms that bees find attractive. The blossoms turn red and start to droop after pollination, signaling the bees to move on to fresher yellow flowers.

Up on the canyon's ridge you'll find bladderpod, an ill-smelling relative of the capers used in cooking. Uncooked, its bladder-shaped pods are poisonous; early natives found them edible when roasted. You may spot some of the elaborately colored harlequin beetles who call the bladderpod home.

After the spring flowers fade, the slopes here turn brown and dry, waiting for a rejuvenating rain. October brings white-crowned sparrows; their

Wild cucumber

thin whistles are a sure sign that fall is here, even if it's 90 degrees out. Year-round, look for brown towhees, lesser goldfinches, and quail.

From the ridge, take the fire road left and uphill, circling the mesa, passing the houses at Parkview Terrace and pausing at the top for a fine view of the bay, the Ocean Beach pier, the downtown skyline, and the Coronado Bridge. Make your way back by taking the path straight downhill, turning right along the canyon's rim.

There's a confusing number of paths leading down to the canyon, some of them quite steep. Look for the concrete rubble across the way, and pick one of the paths just beyond for an easier descent.

7 MISSION BAY: ONCE AROUND THE PARK

LOCATION
Pacific Beach/Mission Beach.

For Walk 1: Take I-5 to Pacific Beach. Go west to Lamont Street, turn left and continue, crossing Crown Point Drive, to the first parking lot (TG1247:J2).

For Walk 2: Take Mission Boulevard south to Santa Clara Point. Park where you can (TG1267:J1).

For Walk 3: From Mission Boulevard, turn left onto West Mission Bay Drive. Then turn right at Quivira Road and into the parking lot (TG1268:A3).

For Walk 4: From I-5, take Sea World Drive west to South Shores Drive. Turn right into the parking area (TG1268:D3).

HOURS
Always open.

DESCRIPTION
Covering 4600 acres of land and water, Mission Bay is said to be the largest aquatic park in the U.S. There are grassy picnic areas, playgrounds, sandy beaches, boat launch facilities, and restrooms all around the bay, as well as resort hotels, marinas, and, of course, Sea World. Mission Bay is a popular destination for tourists and residents alike, especially on weekends and during the summer. Try to come at quieter times. For guided walks and special programs, call (619) 221-8901.

HISTORY
The area now called Mission Bay was once a broad lagoon where Kumeyaay came to hunt waterfowl and gather shellfish. It was deep enough to seem a good port to explorer Sebastian Vizcaino when he arrived in 1602.

Over the next two centuries, things changed. The San Diego River, flowing through on its way to the sea, left the bay choked with sediment, a place of shoals and sandbars known to nineteenth-century sailors as False Bay. Dikes built to keep San Diego Harbor from suffering the same fate only added to False Bay's problems. Fifty years ago it was a large stagnant pond, often used as a trash dump.

When postwar federal funding enabled the building of a flood control channel, the bay was dredged completely, given a new name, and reborn as one of the beauty spots of San Diego.

THE WALKS

With 17.5 miles of flat paved walkways, it's possible to circle the bay's perimeter in half a day. We did it, and we're glad! If you want something shorter, we've broken the circuit into segments.

Walk 1—Feathers to Fossils: Crown Point Shores to La Cima

Distance: 2 miles round trip. *Time:* 45 minutes to 1 hour.

To get some idea of what the area looked like in the old days, start at the fenced Kendall-Frost Marsh Reserve, 16 acres of salt marsh at the east end of the Crown Point Drive parking lot.

Walk along Crown Point Drive to the overlook with its interpretive signs. You can spend a few quiet moments trying to identify some of the 107 bird species that congregate here.

This is a good place to see black skimmers, the black-and-white, orange-legged tropical birds that decided, as other visitors have, that temperate San Diego was a fine spot to settle down and raise their young. In the past twenty-five years, they've increased their numbers to more than 500. They owe their name to their habit of feeding by skimming over the water, dragging their long lower bills along the surface to pick up small fish and shellfish.

Other shorebirds you can pick out of the feathered crowd are curlews, brown with long, down-curving bills, and marbled godwits, also brown, but with straight, two-tone bills that are slightly upturned, as if pointing up to God.

When you're through birding, pick up the paved path near the water heading west, passing under the Ingraham Street bridge and heading toward Sail Bay, popular with weekend sailors.

Just before La Cima Drive and the second set of concrete steps leading up to the street, look for 200,000-year-old sand dollars sticking out from the eroding cliffside. These fossils are similar to the sand dollars found on our beaches today, but, not unexpectedly, a little more worn and fragile.

You can continue walking around Sail Bay, past the Catamaran Hotel, and on to the Bayside Walk.

Fossils at Mission Bay

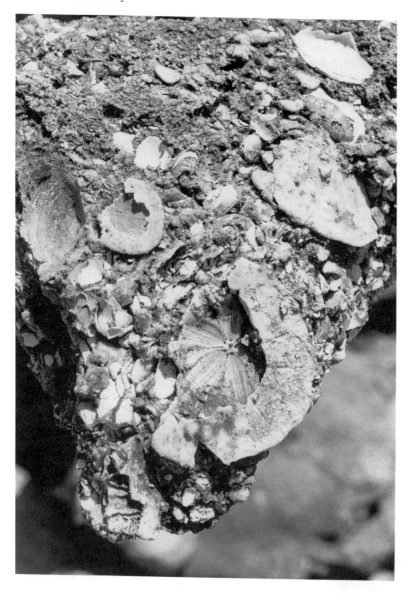

Walk 2—Bayside Walk: Verona Court to the Jetty

Distance: 4 miles round trip. *Time:* 1.5 hours.

Park if you can on Mission Boulevard, or 0.5 mile ahead at Santa Clara Point, where you can rent boats, take lessons in all kinds of water sports, or just stretch out on the grass. The paved and generally peaceful Bayside Walk crosses West Mission Bay Drive, where you may want to stop in at Belmont Park, on the west side of Mission Boulevard.

In 1925, this was the site of an amusement park built by John D. Spreckels, the millionaire sugar king who owned, among other things, most of Coronado Island, two of San Diego's three newspapers, a water supply company, and the "Impossible Railroad," the SDA&E, connecting San Diego to the East Coast. The park featured a large indoor swimming pool called The Plunge and a roller coaster called The Giant Dipper. The area was reborn as a shopping center in 1988, with The Plunge remodeled and reopened. A state historical landmark, the old wooden roller coaster was fully restored in 1990 and is open daily year-round.

Here, on the ocean side of the street, you can take advantage of the paved beachfront promenade for biking, skating, walking, and people watching. Head north to Crystal Pier or south to the jetty, but don't expect to have the path to yourself, especially in warm weather.

Just across from Belmont Park, on the corner of Mission Boulevard and West Mission Bay Drive, is Bonita Cove, whose grassy hill is nice for picnics, kite flying, or frisbee-tossing. It's another mile along the Bayside Walk to the jetty, where you can watch boats coming through the channel or continue your walk along the ocean.

NOTE: Don't even *think* of bringing your car to Mission Boulevard on a sunny weekend afternoon. You'll be stuck in traffic for hours!

Walk 3—Seafood to Seabirds: Quivira Basin

Distance: 2 miles round trip. *Time:* 45 minutes to 1 hour.

When you're in the mood for a seafood lunch, a bike or boat rental, a few hours of sportfishing or whalewatching, or just a quiet dockside walk, drive east on West Mission Bay Drive and turn right into the parking lot at Quivira Road. (For determined nondrivers, there are sidewalks and bike lanes along West Mission Bay Drive.)

Stroll past the boat slips and the restaurants and shops of Marina Village to Hospitality Point, headquarters of Mission Bay Park, where you'll find good birding in the flood control channel. Look for cormorants, pelicans, and, in winter, visiting loons. The oldest living birds on earth, loons have managed to survive, even though they can't walk on land and need at least 0.25 mile of water runway to get themselves airborne. You'll see them swimming low in the water, keeping an ancient eye out for fish.

Walk 4—Kites and Windsurfers: East Mission Bay
Distance: 6 miles round trip. *Time:* 1.5 to 2 hours.

Last but not least, try a long, leisurely walk from the boat launch at South Shores and Sea World Drive to De Anza Cove, passing broad grassy areas, the Hilton Hotel, a number of little beaches, and the Visitor Information Center. On weekends, kite enthusiasts gather at Tecolote Shores, filling the air with flying fish, birds, and dragons. Windsurfers like to launch their bright-colored sailboards near the Information Center, and *everybody* seems to like to picnic on this side of the bay.

If you prefer, you can walk north to south, parking at De Anza Cove, and heading toward man-made Fiesta Island, left in its "natural" state, where the annual Over-The-Line Tournament, a wild and crazy kind of three-man (or woman) softball, is held.

CABRILLO NATIONAL MONUMENT

LOCATION
Point Loma. Take I-5 to Rosecrans (Highway 209) and go south. At Cañon, turn right; continue to Catalina Boulevard and turn left. Catalina soon becomes Cabrillo Memorial Drive. Pass through Fort Rosecrans National Cemetery and continue on to the parking area near the visitor center (TG1308:A2).

HOURS
9:00 A.M. to 5:15 P.M. Parking fee at the visitor center. Tidepool Area, 9:00 A.M. to 4:30 P.M.; no fee.

DESCRIPTION
San Diego's first national monument, Cabrillo is a beautiful place indeed, with sweeping views of San Diego Bay and the Pacific Ocean. There are tidepools to explore, an old lighthouse to visit, and several scenic nature trails to follow. The visitor center has a small historical museum, daily talks, slide shows and films, and an excellent bookshop. You can picnic and bay-watch between the visitor center and the parking lot, or at tables in the grove between the lot and the old lighthouse. Snack and drink

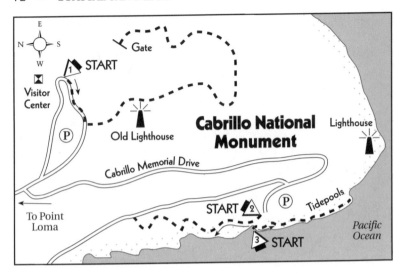

machines and, of course, restrooms can be found at the visitor center.

Cabrillo offers ranger-led nature, tidepool, and military history walks, and in winter, special talks and films on the gray whale migration. Check the bulletin board outside the auditorium, or call (619) 557-5450 for schedules.

HISTORY

Long before Cabrillo's time, Kumeyaay Indians lived on Point Loma. But the monument is named for the Portuguese navigator who sailed under the Spanish flag and had served with Cortez in Mexico. Hoping to find a shortcut to China, Juan Rodriguez Cabrillo sailed northward in June 1542, arriving at San Diego Bay on September 28. He landed near Ballast Point, naming the area San Miguel in honor of Saint Michael, whose feast day it was. Six days later, he sailed north again, and broke a leg going ashore at the Channel Islands. Gangrene set in, and within a few weeks he was dead.

The Old Point Loma Lighthouse, built in 1854, was in operation until 1891, when it was replaced by the lighthouse near the tidepools. More than 450 feet above sea level, the old lighthouse was so high that its light was often obscured by fog and low clouds. During World War II, when Point Loma was the backbone of San Diego's coastal defense system, it was used as a military radio station. In 1913, the lighthouse and the quarter acre of land around it were declared a national monument, commemorating

Statue of Juan Rodriguez Cabrillo

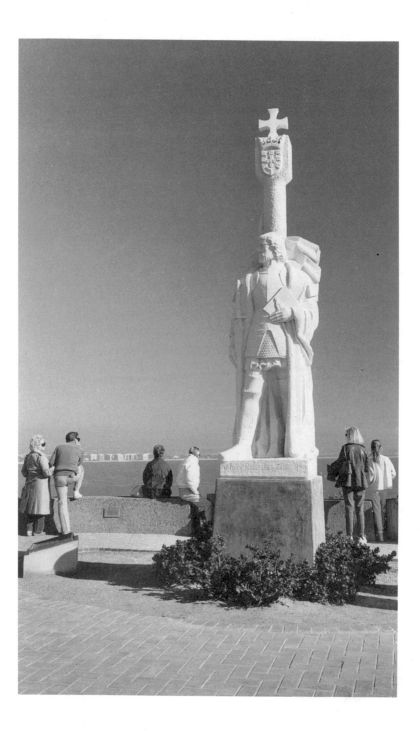

Europe's discovery of the West Coast. Since then, the park has grown to 144 acres, and is, after the Statue of Liberty, the second most visited national monument in the U.S.

Walk 1—Bayside Trail
Distance: 3 miles round trip. *Time:* 1.5 hours.

Follow the sidewalk heading south toward the old lighthouse. At about 0.2 mile you'll notice a paved service road leading downhill to your left; stay on the marked shoulder for another 0.3 mile and take the gravel path on the left. This is the actual start of the Bayside Trail.

Once a military patrol road, the trail winds down the eastern slope of

Old Lighthouse at Cabrillo National Monument

Point Loma with great views all the way. During World War II, Point Loma was honeycombed with bunkers, cannons, and mortars to protect the harbor from Japanese attack; you'll see some of the remains along the trail.

There are occasional benches to rest on as you make the 300-foot descent, and, more importantly, as you climb back up. Take your time and enjoy the view; these chaparral-covered slopes will give you an idea of what San Diego looked like when Cabrillo came.

In spring, the hillsides are covered with yellow bush sunflower, sometimes called brown-eyed Susan, and red flashes of monkey flower and Indian paintbrush.

To the south, you'll see a constant parade of naval vessels, pleasure craft, fishing boats, and ocean liners moving in and out of the harbor. On clear days, you can see Mexico's Coronado Islands and some of the more elegant homes of Tijuana's Las Playas section. Often, there are Navy jets leaving or landing on North Island; a display outside the visitor center will help you identify planes and ships, if you're so inclined.

After the large bunker, look for traces of a 50-million-year-old streambed that flowed into the sea when water still covered the land. The rounded "plug" of grayish mudstone is even older than the surrounding yellow sandstone—about 2 million years older. A few yards below is a break in the rock that indicates an earthquake fault.

At low tide, watch for pelicans, cormorants, and, sometimes, sea lions basking on the rocks of the jetty. Continuing on, you'll see San Diego's skyline and the mountains beyond. At the trail's end, about a mile from the trailhead, you can look ahead to Ballast Point, the slim finger of land where Cabrillo probably landed. Its name comes from its use as a ballast dump for nineteenth-century sailing ships, which used rocks, sand, and dirt to balance the weight of their cargo. Many of the paving stones for San Diego's streets came from here, as did many of the seeds of introduced plants like hottentot fig, tree tobacco, and wild radish, which came with the ballast and stayed on to sprout and reproduce wherever they ended up.

Today, at Ballast Point, you can still see Navy ships and nuclear-powered submarines. Turn around at the gated fence and follow the trail back up to the visitor center. If you're still in the mood, try another walk.

Walk 2—Seaside Trail
Distance: 2 miles round trip. *Time:* 45 minutes.

Just before you come to the main parking area, there's a paved road on your right that leads downhill to the Coast Guard lighthouse and the

Point Loma sewage treatment plant. To your left at the bottom is a small parking lot. From it, you can pick up one of the trails that meander around the bluffs on the west side of Point Loma, overlooking the Pacific Ocean.

Start at the north side of the parking lot. Take the steps down to the bottom, then curve right around the gully and look for the trail heading uphill; the trail to your left leads down to the tidepools (Walk 3). Here on the cliff's edge, you can have good views of the sea and the occasional cormorant or gull flying by. Up here, you're higher than they are!

In spring, look for poppies, deerweed, lupines, and other familiar wildflowers, dwarfed, as are all the plants on this side, by the constant salt spray and sea breezes. At about 0.7 mile, you'll see the rare Shaw's agave, a short, broad succulent that looks like the top of a large pineapple. Soon you'll start heading up toward the road; a good turnaround point is the sign prohibiting the taking of specimens, about 1 mile from the parking lot.

Walk 3—Tidepool Walk
Distance: 1 mile round trip. *Time:* 1 to 2 hours.

On low tide days, especially in fall and winter, don't miss Cabrillo's fine tidepools (see "Exploring Tidepools," under "Walking Shorts").

This walk begins at the same parking lot as Walk 2. Starting at the north side of the parking lot, take the steps down to the bottom, then curve right around the gully and look for the trail heading uphill; the trail to your left leads down to the tidepools and east around the point.

Go out on a descending tide and be prepared to get your feet wet; the best finds are around the point, about 0.5 mile from where you start. You'll have to do some wading to get there. Remember: Look but don't take, and if you've never been tidepooling before, try to arrange your visit to coincide with one of the ranger-led walks.

9 TIJUANA RIVER VALLEY

LOCATION
Imperial Beach.

Tijuana River National Estuarine Research Reserve
Take I-5 south to Coronado Avenue in Imperial Beach. Go west. Coronado Avenue becomes Imperial Beach Boulevard at 13th Street.

For Walk 1: Turn left at the unobtrusive church, St. Mary's by the Sea, on the corner of 5th Street. Drive south a few blocks and park at Iris Street (TG1349:F2).

For Walk 2: Turn left on 3rd Street and right on Caspian Way. Park in the visitor center lot (TG1349:F1).

For Walk 3: Turn left on Seacoast Drive; continue to the end (TG1349:E2).

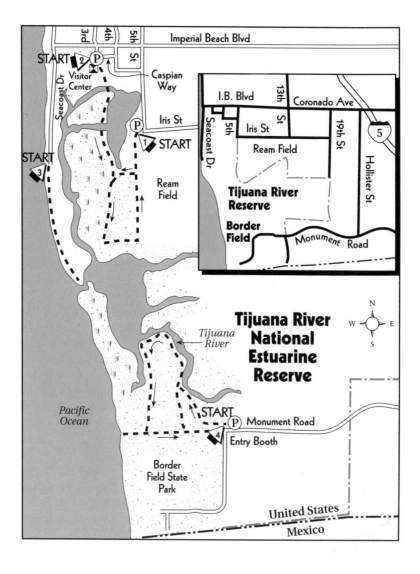

Border Field State Park

For Walk 4: Take I-5 south to the Coronado Avenue exit. Cross Coronado and continue south on Hollister Street. At Monument Road turn right, go to the end, and park by the entry booth (TG1349:G6).

HOURS

Tijuana River National Estuarine Research Reserve: Sunrise to sunset. The visitor center is open daily, 10:00 A.M. to 5:00 P.M. For information, call (619) 575-3613. Border Field State Park: Daily 9:30 A.M. to 5:00 P.M.

DESCRIPTION

Although known officially, since 1982, as the Tijuana River National Estuarine Research Reserve, old-timers still call it the Slough. Southern California's largest remaining estuary and wetland, it covers about 2500 acres of wetland and upland habitats, including the Tijuana Slough National Wildlife Refuge and Border Field State Park.

Most of the water that drains into the Tijuana River comes from Mexico, but the entire estuary is within the U.S. More than 370 species of birds frequent the reserve, finding plenty of shellfish, worms, and fish for food. Several endangered species—the least tern, brown pelican, savannah sparrow, least Bell's vireo, clapper rail, and peregrine falcon—can be found here. Since flooding is common, the days just after a rainstorm are not a good time to come. There are picnic tables, barbecues, and restrooms at Border Field State Park, and restrooms at the visitor center on Caspian Way.

HISTORY

On very old maps this area was known as the Oneonta Slough. Its fertile river valley was the site of a colony of cooperative farmers founded by utopian idealist William E. Smythe near what is now San Ysidro. Calling themselves "Little Landers," 129 families, each with a little land of their own, raised poultry, goats, and produce. They had their own school, library, and community center. They prospered until early 1916, when the flood attributed to rainmaker Charles Hatfield covered their fields with tons of mud and sand (see Lake Morena Park, Chapter 35). By 1918, the colony had disbanded.

Later, parts of the river valley became a sewage dump. During World War II, military installations were built to protect the coast from enemy attack. A small railroad dragged targets out across the dunes for machine gun practice. Ream Field, named for the army's first flight surgeon, Major William Roy Ream, is still used by naval helicopters to practice landings and air-sea rescues.

TIJUANA RIVER NATIONAL ESTUARINE RESEARCH RESERVE

Walk 1—The River Mouth Trail

Distance: 2.5 miles round trip. *Time:* 1.5 hours.

This is the boundary between the reserve and Ream Field, where on weekdays, you can see—and hear—more helicopters than anywhere outside of *Apocalypse Now.*

Enter at the "National Reserve" sign, following the wide path along the boundary fence. At about 0.75 mile, head west toward the river mouth, leading into great birding territory. There are usually dozens of terns, gulls, sandpipers, egrets, ducks, and pelicans down by the river.

In the marshy lowlands, you'll see pickleweed, alkali heath, and taller stands of cordgrass, all typical of our salt marshes. In the mudflats, at low tide, there are cockles, fiddler crabs, and horn snails, whose shells look like tiny cornucopias. The tidal creeks are home to a number of small fish, like silvery top smelt and anchovies, much loved by terns and pelicans. Larger halibut and croaker come here to spawn.

Above the drier uplands, covered with buckwheat, sagebrush, and lemonade berry, look for marsh hawks, also called harriers, easily identified by their white rump spots.

From the river mouth, take the same path back, or make a circle by following the wide trail that angles across the marsh. This will take you past several ponds once used for sand and gravel mining, now home to many kinds of water birds, including the uncommon little blue heron. After about 1.5 miles, you have to double back to connect up with the wide fence-side path bordering Ream Field.

Walk 2—The McCoy Trail

Distance: 2 miles round trip. *Time:* 1 hour.

The trail, named for local environmentalists Mike and Patricia McCoy, who were instrumental in preserving this wetland, leads out from the visitor center into the marsh. On the left side of the path is a cordgrass meadow that looks like an overgrown lawn. Thriving in the tidal ebb and flow, cordgrass is the preferred habitat of endangered clapper rails, secretive marsh birds that use the grass to hide in and to construct their nests. In 1983, storms pushed the barrier sand dunes into the tidal creeks, preventing salt water from coming in, and killing the cordgrass. Predictably, the clapper rails disappeared. Since cordgrass was reintroduced and a new slough created to improve tidal flow, the birds are back; nearly 100 have been counted.

You can walk as far as the second tidal channel and birdwatch a bit before heading back to the visitor center, which has a number of interesting, interactive exhibits. For guided walks and special programs, call (619) 575-3613.

Cordgrass, Tijuana Slough (Photo by Julie Bubar)

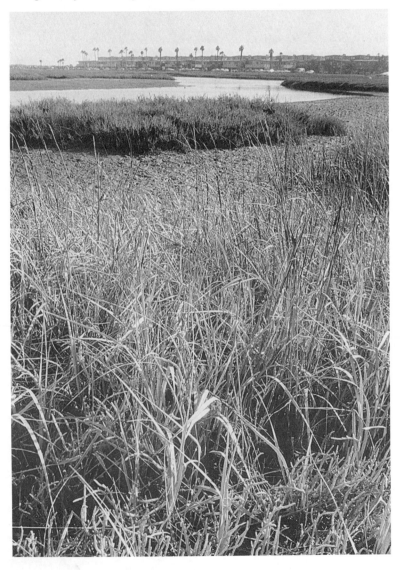

Walk 3—The Beach Walk
Distance: 2 miles round trip. *Time:* 1 hour.

Start at the observation deck at the end of Seacoast Drive and walk south along the beach, past the summer nesting grounds of the endangered least terns. Thousands of these small birds used to nest in San Diego County, scraping shallow nests in the sand in June and July and standing over the eggs to shade them and keep them cool. As sunbathers increasingly spread out over the beaches, the numbers of least terns declined. Today, there are probably only 2000 pairs left in all of Southern California. The area along the tidal creek is closed to human traffic, so the least terns can breed in peace; the beach side of the dunes is open year-round. Rare snowy plovers, tiny relatives of killdeer, also make their shallow nests in the dunes in summer.

Speaking of things endangered, consider the dunes themselves, which protect the estuary's fragile ecosystem. Dune-growing plants can survive nowhere else. Purple sand verbena, pink sea rocket—related to wild radish—and yellow dune primrose are all low-growing plants that stabilize the sand and provide food and shelter for burrowing insects and the California legless lizard, which looks like a small pale snake. San Diego used to have sand dunes along all of its low-lying beaches; development has bulldozed most of them away.

The storms of 1983 pushed the dunes into the river channel, closing the mouth of the river. The sand was dredged out, and the dunes were rebuilt and replanted; they are now off-limits to walkers.

The walk along the beach is never crowded, and you can look out toward the Coronado Islands, 12 miles offshore. Discovered in 1602 by Sebastian Vizcaino, these islands are now a Mexican wildlife preserve and closed to visitors.

BORDER FIELD STATE PARK
Built in the shadow of Tijuana's Bullring by the Sea, this 400-acre state park stands at the southwestern corner of the United States, with a 360-degree view from Point Loma to Tijuana, including the Coronado Islands. Straddling the border is a pyramid-shaped monument marking the international boundary set here in 1848, after the Treaty of Guadalupe Hidalgo made California American territory.

In 1974, Pat Nixon cut the ribbon at the park's dedication ceremony and immediately crossed the border to shake hands with all the Mexican citizens who were watching the goings-on, much to the dismay of the Secret Service. Today, the fence that separates the two countries stretches out into the ocean. This is not a legal border crossing.

Border Patrol keeps a wary eye on the monument area, a popular place for weekend family picnics. Take a short paved walk around the perimeter of the grassy picnic area and admire the view of the ocean and the hills of Tijuana. Display panels in both English and Spanish describe the estuary and its human and natural history.

The beach here is wide, long, and never crowded. Nice as it looks, though, we don't recommend swimming in the water. All too often, sewage washes up from Mexico. When this happens, the park's main road may be closed. Call (619) 575-3613 to check conditions before starting out.

This is the only beach in the county where horseback riding is allowed; rental horses are available at stables along Hollister Street. Walking or riding, it's just over 2 miles to the mouth of the Tijuana River.

Walk 4—Tidal Creek/Beach Loop

Distance: 2 miles round trip. *Time:* 45 minutes to 1 hour.

Start at the equestrian trail west of the entry booth. This is a flat, easy trail, but even in dry weather, parts of it can be muddy and slippery, so watch your step, and be sure to give riders the right-of-way.

Walk through the coastal isocoma, which we prefer to call by its more descriptive name, goldenbush, and bear left at the first junction. If you're lucky, you may see a jackrabbit or two. They have really large ears and leave bigger droppings than cottontails.

Bear right at the next junction, following the tidal creek. Note the white crust of salt on the ground, left behind by evaporated seawater. In El Niño storm years, this whole area can be submerged. There are acres of pickleweed—green in summer, red-tipped in fall—and clumps of sea lavender, which has tiny white flowers and looks something like baby's breath. The large red-tinged leaves at its base may be covered with crystals of salt. Coastal Indians used to brush the salt off the leaves, and use it to season their food.

Off toward your right, there's a pole topped by a nesting platform where black and white ospreys like to sit. You can usually see kestrels and harriers overhead, and you can't miss the Navy helicopters, circling like motorized marsh hawks. As the path loops back toward the Bullring, look for carpets of iceplant, whose small white flowers are followed by magenta seed pods that turn brown in winter. After rain, the succulent leaves begin to grow. Bright green, they may get as big as your hand, but as the flowers start to bloom, they gradually shrink away. Iceplant does have a sort of frosty look, but on closer inspection, you can see that buds and leaves are actually covered with tiny liquid-filled beadlets—the plant's way of storing moisture.

When you come to the beach trail, turn right and head for the ocean. There's a wooden bridge across the revegetated sand dunes, which protected least terns and snowy plovers now call home. Just ahead is one of the nicest stretches of sand in San Diego. You can beach-walk south to the border or north to the river mouth, or spend a few quiet moments pelican-watching before taking the trail straight back to the entry booth.

Part II
INLAND
SAN DIEGO

10 WILDERNESS GARDENS PRESERVE

LOCATION
Pala. Take I-15 north to Highway 76. Go east 10 miles to the entrance of the preserve, on the right about 1 mile past Agua Tibia Ranch, near a sign that says "Rancho Pecaro." Go downhill and park in the designated area (TG409:E6).

HOURS
Open Thursday through Monday, 8:00 A.M. to 4:00 P.M. Closed during August. Parking fee.

DESCRIPTION

This 584-acre county park of mixed woodlands and chaparral is one of our favorite inland destinations. It's a lovely, uncrowded place to walk and picnic, but the only facilities are portapotties and picnic tables (one with handicapped access). Guided tours are sometimes available; call (760) 742-1631.

HISTORY

For centuries before the Spanish came, the area around Pala was an Indian campground; Pala Peak was said to be a sacred spot. In the early 1800s, the padres set up a chapel at Pala as an adjunct to the San Luis Rey Mission, and the land nearby was planted with grain, and also with cotton, to clothe the Indian converts.

Indian reservations were established in the area in the 1870s, despite the protests of local Anglos who thought the land was too good to give away to Indians.

Pala is an Indian word for "water," and the San Luis Rey River still runs through here year-round. In the 1880s, a local miller, M. M. Sickler, diverted the river and used it to power his gristmill. Many Indians, believing that spirits living in the water controlled its flow, were convinced that Sickler had captured one of them and locked him inside the turbine; it was the spirit's desperate struggle to escape that made the mill wheel keep turning.

In the 1950s, Los Angeles publisher Manchester Boddy, founder of Descanso Gardens in La Cañada, bought the acreage for a retirement retreat and named it Wilderness Gardens. He planted 100,000 of his beloved camellias here, and put in five ponds to irrigate them. At present, only one of the ponds has water in it, and only a few camellias remain, but they still put on an impressive springtime display.

After Boddy's death in 1967, the gardens were abandoned and threatened with development. Rescued by Small Wilderness Area Preserves (SWAP), a statewide organization, the preserve was opened to the public as a walk-in facility in 1983.

THE WALKS

Whether you want a short walk or a long one, start at the kiosk near the entrance, where you'll find a large park map and information brochures.

Walk 1 begins just beyond the kiosk. For Walks 2 and 3, take the footbridge across the usually docile river and pick up the trail to your left.

In winter, it's a good idea to call first to see if the river is crossable. Once it had power enough to carve out the gorge here, but that was before it was dammed at Lake Henshaw. Today it's a good place to find crayfish, those miniature lobsters that live only in slow-moving fresh water.

Continue along into the trees—cottonwoods, live oaks, sycamores, and willows—all typical streamside dwellers. You'll notice a lot of poison oak growing in the park; try to notice it from a distance, and don't be attracted by its fall color, as one of our TV newspersons was several years ago, posing for the cameras with a big bouquet of it in her arms.

Walk 1—Alice Fries Nature Trail
Distance: 0.8 mile round trip. *Time:* 20 minutes.

This flat, open trail, a good choice for young children, was named for one of San Diego's finest birders. A virtual Henry Higgins of the bird world, she could listen to white-crowned sparrows in the field and tell where they were born by their accents. She was responsible for the creation of the least tern preserve at Camp Pendleton, wrote a column called "Bird Talk" for a local paper, and inspired hundreds of birders, including one of the authors.

The trail starts to the right of the kiosk and winds through boulders and buckwheat toward the weathered bluffs topped by Highway 76. Keep an eye out for turkey vultures, red-tailed hawks, and rattlesnakes before looping back to the parking lot about 25 yards east of where you began.

Walk 2—The Sensory Trail

Distance: 0.3 mile round trip. *Time:* 15 minutes.

This is soon to be a kind of sensory par course, wheelchair accessible, with signs in Braille for blind visitors and suggested sense-sharpening exercises for others. So far, there are only empty signposts, but things should be completed by the end of 2000.

Go left at the fork and follow the unmarked posts through the coast live oaks, with prickly pear growing among them. In spring, there's a lot of deerweed growing here, with more bees than deer attracted to its small yellow and red flowers.

Tall oaks from little acorns grow, as you can tell along the trail, where you can see them in various stages of development. You can sit on a fallen tree trunk and study the process. As for the fallen tree itself, notice the holes in the bark made by boring insects, which are actually rather interesting insect drillers, helping the dead tree to decompose and enrich the soil.

Bear left at the fork, passing a few small cottonwoods, which will doubtless be big cottonwoods a few years down the road. As you amble on, listen to the wind rustle through the twinkling cottonwood leaves, making a sound like raindrops.

There's another insect phenomenon to watch for: ant-lion pits. At the bottom of each of these small, upside-down volcanoes is an ant-lion larva, or "doodle-bug," waiting for an insect lunch to drop in. The mature ant lion is more like a dragonfly, and flies off in search of its food.

After about 0.1 mile, bear right; you'll see Whipple's yucca and, on your right, a fine specimen of tall, pale Great Basin sage, grayer and larger-leafed than the coastal variety, surrounded by buckwheat.

There are occasional benches where you can sit and admire the many shades of green and, in spring, the colors of purple lupine and golden yarrow.

At the trail's end, head back to the "Upper Meadows Trail" sign and the parking area, or turn left at the trail guide box and pick up Walk 3.

Walk 3—Upper Meadows Trail

Distance: 2.5 miles round trip. *Time:* 1.5 to 2 hours.

From the first left fork, follow the trail sign and bear right at the trail guide box. In fall, look for acorns on the ground; the slim pointy ones are live oaks, or will be some day.

Listen for acorn woodpeckers; they sound like rusty bedsprings, if you're old enough to remember what that sounds like. Look for holly-leaf cherry, with its notched leaves and dark brown summer fruits that are more pit than cherry. Its Latin name is *Prunus ilicifolia,* which sounds more like a prune or a plum; Indians called it *islay,* and ate it.

You'll see plenty of coyote droppings as you walk along, but it's unlikely that you'll see the generally nocturnal coyotes. Keep an eye out for the usual lizards, squirrels, and quail.

At about 0.3 mile, there's a toyon, or California holly, with narrower leaves than the holly-leaf cherry, and yellow berries that start forming in summer, turning to bright red by late October. Just ahead is a large clump of yellow broom, a mass of color when it blooms in early fall, and prettier than the more common coastal variety.

At about 0.5 mile, you start to climb uphill. This is usually a good place to listen for the "voice of the chaparral," the wren tit, singing in the scrub higher up.

As you climb, notice the green woodland ferns on the hillsides; even in the middle of summer, there's a cool, woodsy feeling here. You'll soon find yourself on a ridge looking out across the valley to the mountains, at the foot of which is yet another sand and gravel company, busily grinding up the terrain to make new foundations. Closer at hand, just below you, is a corner of the stone mill that Sickler built 100 years ago.

The trail continues to climb, with wooden steps to help you. There's a short section—only about 25 feet—where you might appreciate a walking stick; you'll certainly want good treads on your shoes.

Then you're at the top of the mesa, with a 360-degree view. You can look down on one of the ponds put in by publisher Boddy to irrigate his camellias. It's the only one that's currently full of water and visited by ringnecked and ruddy ducks.

Circle around a dry pond and head down to the wet one. Notice that, up here, you're back in chaparral country, where it's drier and hotter. The streamside vegetation is down below, near the river.

Tiptoe through the buckwheat, and past a meadow. In fall, everything here looks reddish—buckwheat, sumac flowers, soil, and rocks. After all that restful green, it's strange to be walking through the buckwheat's red glare.

At about a mile, you start descending again. Cross a log footbridge and come face to face with a good-sized toyon. If you're ready for more climbing, follow the sign just ahead on your left to the Upper Meadows and Pala Peak; it's about another mile to the west, and you'd do well to carry some water along.

We head east down to the pond and back to the woodlands. In winter, there could be water running alongside the trail; in spring, the area is covered with wild cucumber, hairy-flowered clematis vines, and scarlet heart-leaf penstemon.

At just over a mile, there's a dead oak trunk, still standing, pocked with the storage holes of acorn woodpeckers, which usually prefer the softer wood of sycamores.

At about 1.3 miles, you come out at the dirt road that circles the fishing pond. Straight ahead is a willow-shaded, pond-side picnic table, if you're ready for lunch. If you're not picnicking, go left, heading around the pond and crossing an earthen dam. You'll see grapes, willows, mulefat, and horehound fringing the water, and cattails in it. Wilderness Gardens is no place to rush through, and you'll probably have it all to yourself, especially on weekdays.

Follow the dirt road toward the river. Turn right, keeping the river to your left as you head back to your car.

11 GUAJOME REGIONAL PARK

LOCATION
Vista. Take I-5 north to Highway 76, and go east about 7 miles.

For Walk 1: Turn right at Guajome Lake Road, then right to the park's main entrance (TG1067:D7).

For Walk 2: Turn right at North Santa Fe Avenue, then left to the park's lower entrance (TG1087:D1).

HOURS
9:30 A.M. to 5:00 P.M. weekdays, 9:30 A.M. to sunset weekends. Parking fee.

DESCRIPTION
An attractive 569-acre county park in a part of the county that isn't as rural as it used to be, Guajome is still a good spot to picnic, walk, or camp. Fishermen enjoy the spring-fed, man-made lakes, and the marshy habitats are popular with birds and birders. There are a number of picnic tables and barbecues, a playground, and a camping area. For reservations, call County Parks, (858) 565-3600. You can also visit the historic adobe or the Antique Steam and Gas Engine Museum nearby (see "By the Way . . ." below).

HISTORY
The Indians who inhabited the area around Guajome were called Luiseños by the padres after the building of San Luis Rey Mission in 1798. The land was used for grazing and growing grain until the missions were secularized nearly half a century later. Guajome, an Indian word for "home of the frog,"

was one of the few land grants actually assigned to Indians—two brothers who soon sold all 2200 acres for $500 to an L.A. merchant, Abel Stearns. He gave it as a wedding present to his young sister-in-law, Ysadora Bandini, and her new husband, Cave Couts.

Couts, a Tennessean who graduated from West Point with Ulysses S. Grant, was an army colonel and a kind of nineteenth-century "good ole boy." Transferred to San Diego, he stayed at the home of the wealthy Don Juan Bandini, went into business with him, and married his beautiful daughter in 1851.

With the help of 300 Luiseños, the thirty-room adobe ranch house was built, landscaped, and fortified against attack by less tractable Indians. Charged with murder more than once, but always acquitted, Couts had good connections. He was given a judgeship and became a subagent for the Indians of San Diego County, helping to determine their fates.

He and his wife raised ten children, two of whom died and are said to be buried under the large aloe tree to the left of the chapel door. The Coutses had hundreds of sheep and cattle and were known for their expansive hospitality.

Some guests posed special problems. It is said that U. S. Grant was asked to leave when he rode his horse into the dining room, and Helen Hunt Jackson, author of *Ramona*, the Indians' *Uncle Tom's Cabin*, tried to stir up an Indian revolt on the property and had to be locked in her room.

After Couts died, his son remodeled the house, married a niece of Mark Twain, and continued the tradition of hospitality. The guests kept on coming, even after the marriage ended. Until his death in 1943, Cave Couts, Jr., liked to be known as the "last of the Dons."

His common-law son lived here until the property was condemned. The county paid him a million dollars for the house and the 165 acres of surrounding land. The park was opened to the public in 1973. The adobe was declared a national monument, and underwent major restoration in 1996.

Walk 1—The Nature Trail
Distance: 2 miles round trip. *Time:* 1 hour.

Park opposite the restrooms and follow the paved walkway around, past the playground and picnic areas. Pepper trees and newly planted sycamores line the path, and there's usually a whole lot of quackin' going on down by the water—you may want to bring along some bread to feed the ducks and geese that congregate here. These are a motley crew, offspring of unwanted domestic ducks and wild mallards, and are always hungry.

Where the pavement ends, near the information kiosk, turn right and follow the lakeside path through rows of tall casuarinas, pine-like trees imported from Australia. The straight rows of holes in the trunks are made by red-breasted sapsuckers, which make daily visits to the holes to eat the insects that have been attracted to the sap and trapped there.

At about 0.25 mile, take the right-hand path past the cattails and tules alongside the water. Tules, by the way, is pronounced "too-lees," not "tools." "Out in the tules" is an old local expression for out in the sticks, but recent development has caught up with most of our tules.

In late spring, look for marsh mallows here—not the toastable ones, but a kind of low-growing hollyhock. In winter, after rain, the trail here can get pretty muddy—this is real adobe underfoot. In hot weather, the ground is as parched and cracked as dry clay, which is exactly what it is.

Soon you'll reach the marked section of the trail, which, as is often our habit, we prefer to take backwards. Start at marker #15, a large clump of mallow, tules, and bristly ox-tongue, whose leaves look something like their name but whose flowers look more like dandelions.

Bear right at #15, then, almost immediately, left at #14—some prickly pear cacti. As you cross the willow-shaded bridge, see if you can spot any tadpoles in the water. Remember, Guajome means "home of the frog"; you may see some full-grown bullfrogs or bright green California tree frogs here, especially in summer.

After the bridge, turn left. There are clumps of mistletoe in the black willows here, and crested phainopeplas in the mistletoe, especially when the autumn berries start appearing. Phainopeplas, also called silky flycatchers, look like black cardinals—at least the males do. The females and young are gray, but all have white wing patches, visible when flying, and red eyes.

In spring, the maturing seed pods of the black willows look like fluffed-out cotton balls. Sometimes there's so much fluff hanging from the branches, it seems almost like snow (remember snow?). You can feel the tiny seeds inside each cottony wad. If you have hay fever, just walk on by; this stuff can make you sneeze.

Soon you'll have to cross over a fallen tree. Look for celery growing just underneath—it has leaves like Italian parsley and tiny white spring flowers. If you're not sure it's celery, squeeze a stalk between your fingers and see if it smells like the store-bought stuff.

There are occasional tree trunks and branches crossing the path from here on, so you'll have to do a bit of ducking and dodging. At #11, there are stinging nettles, with large, long-stemmed notched leaves—don't try squeezing them. Every part of these plants is covered with stinging hairs that contain the same formic acid found in ants. In the old days, Indians beat rheumatism sufferers with nettle switches to try to ease their pain; it sounds a little like trading a headache for an upset stomach. We know a woman who once answered a call of nature in a clump of nettles and was truly sorry for hours afterwards. Some people say you can boil the leaves, and eat them like spinach. We've never felt like trying.

Duck down again up ahead, but don't lift your head too soon; there are two trunks to clear. If it weren't for the unmistakable sounds of traffic nearby, you'd feel as if you were in the middle of a forest.

As you cross the next wooden bridge, listen for a *kek-kek-kek-kek* in the tules, which means there's a Virginia rail nearby. Grayish-brown, with an orange bill, the Virginia rail is a secretive bird; you'd have to be pretty sharp to spot one. You're more likely to see blackbirds—red-winged, tricolored, and yellow-headed ones—sometimes whole flocks of them out after flying insects.

There's more celery just past #8; then the trail forks left toward the camping area. Unless you're in a hurry to get back, keep to the right and on the nature trail. Up ahead, shaded by willows, is a clump of yerba mansa, which blooms in May and June. Its large white "petals" are really leaves; the yellow cone-shaped centers are the actual flowers. The name in Spanish means "gentle or tame herb"; it's called the "herb of the tame Indian" because Mission Indians used it so often as a general painkiller and for poultices.

Duck again and go on. Ahead on the left is #3, a narrow-leafed willow.

Farther along on the right is another #3, the more common black willow; a non-native fan palm has staked out a nice shady spot here. To complete your comparative willow study, check out #1, the arroyo willow. Tall as it is, it's not considered a tree, since it has more than one trunk.

You're now at the main service road. To get back to where you started, bear left, then right. Walk uphill, keeping the campground to your right. At the crossroads there, head downhill and back through the casuarinas to the parking lot.

Walk 2—The Back-to-Nature Trail

Distance: 3.5 miles round trip. *Time:* 1.5 to 2 hours.

This horse trail can get hot in summer, but we love it, since it gives a real sense of the way things used to be. Start at the park's alternate entrance on North Santa Fe Avenue, taking the main service road just south of the parking spaces and walking in a few feet to pick up the equestrian trail. Head right toward the houses, alongside a marshy meadow. The fennel forest here attracts black-and-yellow butterflies called anise swallowtails. They lay their eggs on the fennel, which becomes a food supply for the voracious black-and-yellow-striped green caterpillars. While fennel—or anise—is their food of choice, these caterpillars will eat their way through anything in the carrot family.

Despite the occasional houses on the hillsides, you still get a wonderful rural feeling here—so far. Look for hawks and kites, as well as ring-necked pheasants, probably descendants of an exotic bird farm once located nearby. These Asian imports are some of the most colorful birds in San Diego; their bodies and long tail feathers are iridescent bronze, and their green heads are set off by red eye patches and white neck rings.

At about 0.6 mile, in the rock outcropping on your right, you can see ferns, mosses, and lichens after the first winter rains. As you continue on, you'll pass several elderberry trees, whose purple fruit has long been a favorite of home winemakers.

Turn right at the fork in the trail at 0.75 mile, heading uphill through coastal sage scrub. After a few hundred feet, there's a short side trail to your left leading to a shady glade where you can sit on a rock secluded from the world, surrounded by hemlock, elderberry, willows, and poison oak. You might see a gopher poking his head up from the ground; you'll certainly hear the sound of water not far away. In fall, there are wild grapes—look for the tangled vines.

From here, an overgrown bit of path leads toward a small waterfall you can't quite get to. You'll be stopped by a dense hedge of wild roses—

and a lot of poison oak. Back on the trail, you'll soon come to the cattail-fringed upper pond. There are houses on the hill up ahead, but you'll lose them as you start circling the pond, seeing only hilltop stables and greenhouses and, way off to the east, snow-capped mountains, a bit of a surprise on a hot winter's day.

At 1.5 miles, you'll reach the top of North Santa Fe Avenue. Turn left quickly and follow the trail back out of civilization and into the tules.

Notice the freshwater clamshells scattered near the creek crossing, the remains of many raccoon dinners. Ahead, the trail is lined with mustard and wild radish, and the country scents of fennel and horse manure perfume the air. Just before 2 miles, take the high road, bearing right. Where the road forks again, bear left, and as the trail rises, near the old fence, left again. You'll be heading back, somewhat steeply, downhill—watch your step.

At 2.5 miles, cross the willow-shaded creek to some nice sittable rocks, perfect for picnics. Here, in winter, you can watch the willows bud. If you stay long enough—a few weeks or so—you'll see the "pussy willows" turn to green or yellow catkins, followed by fluffy seeds. Even if you don't plan to picnic, this is a lovely rest stop.

Continuing on, turn right at the next fork, and cross the creek again; wild roses bloom here in spring. Farther on, watch the open areas for the speedy ground cuckoos called roadrunners. Seen standing still, they're much nobler-looking than their cartoon namesake, with their "Mohawk" crowns, long tails, and red-and-blue eye patches.

Upper Pond, Guajome (Photo by Barbara Moore)

Stay on the main trail, bearing left at the forks. Soon you'll see the ranger residences and campground and, at 3 miles, rejoin the main service road. Go left, passing the head of the nature trail on your right.

As the soil gets saltier, notice the predominance of salt marsh plants, like pickleweed and gray-green Australian salt bush, a favorite perch of meadowlarks. Back in the 1880s, salt bush was introduced as cattle fodder in hope that San Diego's skinny cows could be fattened up enough to make richer milk. The cattle ignored the salt bush and kept producing natural low-fat milk, a century too soon for the anti-cholesterol craze.

Just ahead is the end—and the beginning—of the trail, where picnic tables, restrooms, and your car are all waiting for you.

BY THE WAY. . .

Rancho Guajome Adobe

About 1.5 miles south of the North Santa Fe Avenue park entrance is the "Cadillac of Adobes," built by Cave Couts and his Indian workforce. The entrance is marked by iron gates and county park signs. After a million-dollar restoration project in 1996, the adobe and its beautiful gardens are open for guided tours on weekends. Group tours are also available on weekdays. Admission fee. For details, call (760) 724-4082. (TG1087:G2)

Antique Gas and Steam Engine Museum

The entrance to the museum at 2040 North Santa Fe Avenue is easy to spot; there's a big tractor out front and an even bigger sign. Twice a year, in June and October, the popular Threshing Bee and Antique Engine Show takes place here, demonstrating farm equipment, crafts, and techniques of bygone days. Founded in 1976, the museum includes 40 acres of farmland and more than 1000 different items, and is dedicated to the preservation of the rural ways of early California. It is open daily from 10:00 A.M. to 4:00 P.M. Admission fee. For more information, call (760) 941-1791. (TG1087:G2)

12 DIXON LAKE RECREATION AREA

LOCATION

Escondido. Take I-15 north to El Norte Parkway, then go east to La Honda Drive. Turn north and follow La Honda to the park entrance (TG1110:C3).

HOURS

6:00 A.M. to sunset. Parking fee on weekends.

DESCRIPTION

Owned and operated by the city of Escondido, Dixon Lake is an attractive reservoir surrounded by 527 acres of green grass, rolling hills, and shade trees. There are three picnic areas with tables and barbecues, playgrounds and horseshoe pits, and a campground. Fishing for trout, bass, and catfish is popular; the required state license and day permit are obtainable at the concession near the ranger station.

Rowboats, motorboats, and paddleboats are available for rental, and Dixon Lake has good facilities for the handicapped; restrooms, picnic sites, and the pier near the ranger station all have handicapped access.

A nature trail leads through the primitive section of the grounds. If you like peace and quiet, it's best to avoid summer weekends.

For camping, boating, and group picnic reservations, call (760) 741-3328. For other information, call (760) 839-4680.

HISTORY

Dixon Lake was named for James B. Dixon, son of a failed citrus grower who came to Escondido in the late 1800s and started a new and successful

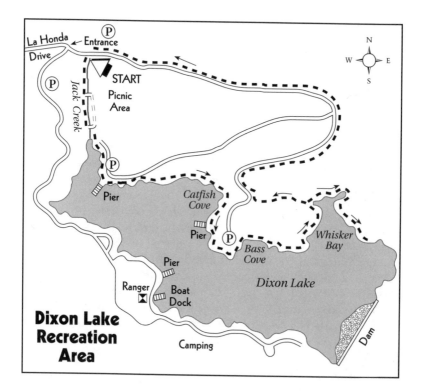

citrus nursery. Known locally as "Mr. Water," Jim Dixon was for many years Superintendent of the Escondido Water Company, and one of the first to envision a reservoir here, close to the small dam at Jack Creek that his father had built to provide more water for his trees.

The site was a good choice, high enough to allow water to flow by gravity, thus eliminating the need for an expensive pumping system. The dam, 100 feet high, was built in 1972; the reservoir was opened to the public in 1977. More than 90 percent of its water comes from the Colorado River.

The Walk
Distance: 3.5 miles round trip. *Time:* 2 hours.

Park in the small lot a few hundred feet from the entrance, or, if this one's full, go through the primitive gate just beyond and park in the lot to your left.

Look for the rock-lined nature trail to the right of the gate; you should find trail guides in a wooden box nearby.

Walk through a grove of acacia trees, covered with yellow flowers in early winter and stringbean-like seed pods in spring. Cross the service road and continue on, between picnic areas #1 and #2 and over a small wooden bridge. This is a nice, shady bit of trail, which you'll appreciate if you come on a hot summer day, when the temperature can climb to over 100 degrees.

Ahead is a big rock overhang, which we like to imagine was a shelter for Indians or perhaps the Dixon boys 100 years ago; look at the smoke-blackened walls. There's a bench where you can sit beside the canyon and listen to the waterfall below, just a trickle in summer, more serious after winter rains.

At about 0.3 mile, the trail forks. Go left downhill to the mouth of Jack Creek, named for the jackrabbits that were once plentiful here. Take the steps down, curve left, and cross the wooden bridge over the creek. To the right, just after the crossing, is another bench where you can sit by the water and contemplate the sometime waterfall.

We go left, past mulefat, cattails, and, in fall, bright spots of red California fuchsia. On your right, look for mossy resurrection plant, brown and dead looking in dry seasons until rainfall turns it a lively green.

Continue along, bearing right along the lakeshore and up the wooden erosion control steps. At the top, go right again, unless you've had enough, in which case the left-hand path will lead you back to picnic area #2.

We head on toward the dam, going down a stone stairway, and staying off the vehicle road. Bear left into the trees, and a lovely, shady part of the trail overlooking the green water. There are blackberries trailing down the hillside in fall, and fishermen trying their luck in the lake year-round.

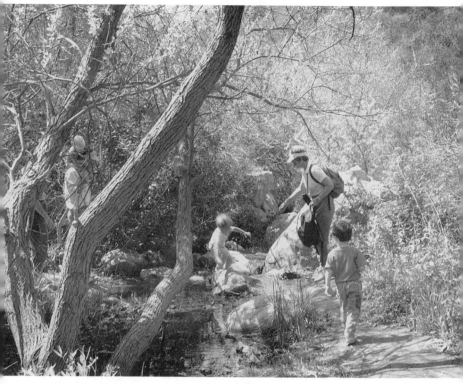

Crossing Jack Creek (Photo by Barbara Moore)

The trail winds up and down through the willows, bypassing a fishing pier. Keep an eye out for the resident osprey that likes to perch on the telephone pole to the right of the dam.

In fall and winter, look for Bonaparte's gulls. They're the only local gull that dives for its dinner; all others are scavengers. Walk between the mauve plumes of fountain grass, and listen for the laughing sound of pied-billed grebes on the lake.

Just over a mile, before you round the turn to the Catfish Cove pier, there's a small grassy area at the water's edge that's perfect for picnics. Even if you're not thinking of food, you might want to sit beside the shoreside willow and the pampas grass and stare at the lake for awhile.

In spring, look for the purple flowers of showy penstemon and, on the hills, lots of blue ceanothus. You can, if you wish, take a detour to the pier; we keep circling the lake.

At about 1.5 miles, there's a broad view of the dam and the mountains behind it, and you start through a drier section of trail, mostly broom and buckwheat. If you're out in the early morning or late afternoon, you might see mule deer on the hillsides; raccoons, coyotes, and the occasional fox or bobcat have been sighted here. Even if you don't get to see any of them, look for their tracks as you walk along.

Circle Whisker Bay, a popular trout-fishing spot fringed with pampas grass. Pass the next left-forking road and walk on, through overhanging sumac and willows, up and down the gentle hills, toward the ultimate portapotty—one with a commanding view of the lake.

Just over 2 miles is as far as you can go. There's another nice picnic spot here, on the flat rocks by the water's edge, just before the buoy line. We're told this is a good place to fish for catfish. Ahead is the 100-year spillway, designed to withstand even our legendary 100-year floods, and the dam.

When you're ready to leave, retrace your steps about 0.2 mile to the end of the "U" of Whisker Bay, and head up to the ridge for a speedy return trip. It won't be as pretty a walk, or as shady, but you will get a bird's-eye view of the lake.

Bear right onto the vehicle road at the top of the trail; the road to your left only leads to a parking lot. If you want a little more lake, you can head downhill farther on and pick up the nature trail again; otherwise, you'll be back at your car in about 20 minutes.

Fishing at Dixon Lake (Photo by Barbara Moore)

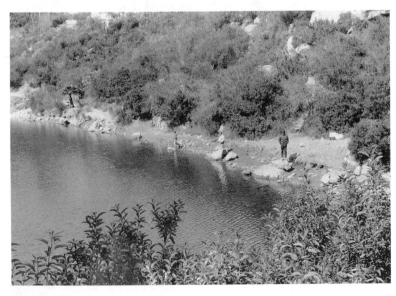

13 DALEY RANCH

LOCATION
Escondido. La Honda Drive (see directions to Dixon Lake, above). Park in the lot just across from the Dixon Lake entrance (TG1110:C3).

HOURS
Sunrise to sunset.

DESCRIPTION
Adjacent to Dixon Lake is this 3058-acre expanse of hills, valleys, and meadows, with more than 20 miles of trails for hikers and bikers to follow. Daley Ranch offers a wide range of walking opportunities, from casual strolls to more challenging treks. On Sundays, a shuttle bus carries visitors to the Ranch House, avoiding the first uphill stretch. There's drinking water at the trailhead and water, picnic tables, portapotties, and telephones at the Ranch House. The trails can get really steamy, so bring extra water. Guided walks and special programs are frequently offered; call Dixon Lake (760) 839-4680 for information.

HISTORY
Indians lived in this area for centuries, but the first European settler was Robert Daley, a young English immigrant who built a small cabin here in 1869. In 1875, he acquired a land grant of 1600 acres, and for years his family farmed and raised horses here and went on buying land all over the county.

After Daley died in 1916, the family moved to Jamul, but continued to use the ranch as a summer retreat. The present Ranch House was built in 1928. In 1996, when the ranch was threatened by development, the city of Escondido voted to buy the land and keep it as a habitat preserve.

The Walk
Distance: 3 miles round trip. Add 3.4 miles for Jack Creek Meadow Loop.
Time: 1.5 to 2.5 hours.

This is our favorite walk here, since it's full of variety and isn't terribly strenuous. Follow the wide paved road uphill from the parking lot, passing through a pleasant oak grove about 0.5 mile in. Note the Englemann oaks, larger-leafed and much less common than coast live oaks. This first part is the most demanding, but there are occasional benches to rest on and a nice mountain vista to enjoy.

Up ahead on your left is the turnoff to the Boulder Loop Trail, a sometimes steep 2.5-mile circuit that rewards you with impressive granite boulders and westward views all the way to the ocean.

Another 0.3 mile on is a green oasis where you'll find the Ranch House. It's fun to wander around the old outbuildings, surrounded by birdsong; more than 100 species have been counted around the preserve, and you can always see a number of them here. Look for acorn woodpeckers in the oak trees; you can see their storage holes pocking the utility poles.

Walk past the outbuildings, take the first right, and the next right will lead 0.5 mile up the Sage Trail to Mallard Lake. Mallard Lake is more a pond than a lake, but it's deep enough to hide the remains of the original log cabin built by Robert Daley. Take the right-forking path halfway around the water; it's the old dam, which made this catchment pond possible.There's a lone Engelmann oak you can rest under, and after that, a good view of two other ponds and the valley and hills beyond.

Back at the Ranch House, if you're still in the mood, look for the Jack Creek Meadow Loop at the north end of the main road; this flat 3.4-mile trail is a perfect choice for families with small children. Follow the willow-fringed creek through the grassy meadow which, in late spring, is bright with tall yellow Hooker's evening primrose, while the drier slopes are carpeted with magenta canchalagua. In summer, you'll see and hear plenty of small, noisy lesser goldfinches; they love the seeds of the purple thistle and the shorter, yellow bristly ox-tongue that lines the trail.

When you're ready to head for your car, try this variation to the main road back, a less-traveled path that snakes around Middle Pond. About 500 feet past the Ranch House, take your first left, heading up the East Trail. At about 0.2 mile, take the second right-forking path, passing through fields of buckwheat, toward the power poles. A bit farther on, when you see the first pond, the path narrows. Bear right, following the path closest to the water, then bear left to rejoin the wider dirt road. Again, bear right toward the water, crossing the dam. Soon you'll be back on the main road, 0.3 mile from the parking lot.

Nature study (Photo courtesy of the San Diego Natural History Museum)

14 ELFIN FOREST RECREATIONAL RESERVE

LOCATION
Escondido. Take I-5 to La Costa Avenue, go east to Rancho Santa Fe Road, and turn left. Turn right on San Elijo Hills Road, and right again on Elfin Forest Road, the first right after the landfill. Elfin Forest Road becomes Harmony Grove Road. The entrance is on your right near the 6-mile marker (TG1149:A1).

HOURS
8:00 A.M. to sunset.

DESCRIPTION
A 750-acre open space park with 10 miles of hiking, biking, and horse trails, Elfin Forest has a flat streamside section and lots of rugged chaparral, with steep ascents and good views as you climb. There are portapotties and drinking fountains in the parking lot. Guided tours are sometimes available. For information, call (760) 753-6466, ext. 146.

HISTORY
A joint effort of the Olivenhain Water District and the Bureau of Land Management (BLM), Elfin Forest Reserve was opened in 1992 as the recreational part of the Olivenhain Water Storage Project. In 1998, the District entered the design phase of a 340-foot-high dam and a 24,000-acre storage

New growth after a fire (Photo courtesy of the San Diego Natural History Museum)

reservoir which will flood the canyons southeast of the reserve. The project is scheduled for completion by the end of 2001.

The Walk—Botanical Trail/Way Up Loop
Distance: 1.5 miles round trip. *Time:* 1 hour.

Go left at the information kiosk to find the Botanical Trail which follows Escondido Creek, a year-round stream that flows from Lake Wohlford in northeast Escondido to the sea. At this writing, there's a lot of habitat restoration going on here, with eucalyptus trees being pulled out and replaced with native live oaks, sycamores, willows, and smaller streamside plants. Just beyond the pretty creek-viewing area is a box of trail guides. To continue the walk you'll have to cross over the creek, which means rock-hopping. If you're not sure of foot, or the water's too high, don't go.

Soon you'll leave the shady streamside greenery for the open chaparral and a steep switchback trail. "Elfin Forest"—the name of a nearby community—is also another name for the short, scrubby shrubs of the chaparral.

This area of the county is prone to fires. Recent fires have left their marks, but black tree skeletons quickly sprout new green additions (see the sidebar "A Word About Chaparral," in Chapter 2).

Look for black-chinned hummingbirds flitting through the scrub oaks, their small bodies a flash of iridescent green. If you get close enough to see a purple throat band, you'll know it's a male.

There are plenty of flowers here in springtime. You'll see red-orange monkey flower, blue lupines and snapdragons, and golden poppies. The maple scent in the air is pearly everlasting; you'll see stalks of its cream-colored flowers all through the summer.

On weekends, this can be a mountain bike freeway. Get here early, and you'll be virtually alone. The Botanical Trail leads into the Way Up Trail; curving left means heading for the Ridge Top Picnic Area, about another mile up. If you're game for a somewhat strenuous climb, keep going; there's no shade at the top, but there are miles of views. Otherwise, turn right, and take the Way Up Trail downhill. There's an easier creek crossing this way, over a cement bridge and back to the parking lot.

Before you leave, take a shady walk along the short Escondido Creek Trail. You can sit on a rock under an oak tree and watch the water flowing to the sea.

15 LAKE HODGES

LOCATION
Del Dios (North Shore).

For Walk 1: Take I-15 north to Via Rancho Parkway; turn left. After several miles, turn left again to Lake Drive. The entrance gate is on Lake Drive between Beech and Ash Lanes, next to the community park. Park in the lot near the concession, about a mile in from the front gate (TG1149:E2).

For Walk 2: From Del Dios Highway, take Rancho Drive down to Lake Drive. Park in the lot across from Hernandez Hideaway (TG1149:E4).

Rancho Bernardo (South Shore).

For Walk 3: Take I-15 to West Bernardo Drive. Exit and turn left. Continue to Community Park Drive, just across from the large retirement home on the hill. Park between the recreation center and the tennis courts. The trailhead is just across the street (TG1150:A6).

For Walk 4: Take West Bernardo Drive south to Duenda; turn right. Duenda becomes Poblado Drive. Park near the trailhead between Smoke Signal Drive and Moon Song Court (TG1149:H7).

HOURS
Open daily, sunrise to sunset. North shore entrance gate open Friday through Sunday, March through October.

DESCRIPTION
A popular spot for fishing, boating, and windsurfing, Lake Hodges is a city reservoir operated by the San Diego Water Utilities Department. For

landlubbers, there are picnic tables and portapotties strategically located around the lake, which is part of the San Dieguito River Park Trail System, the Coast-to-Crest Trails that will eventually go from the beach at Del Mar all the way to Volcan Mountain, a distance of 55 miles. Even on weekdays and in winter when the lake is closed, walkers are welcome; just park outside the gate. There are restrooms and drinking fountains near the North Shore concession, and at the Rancho Bernardo Community Center and Senior Center on the South Shore. For lake information, call (619) 465-3474. For guided walk schedules, call the River Park, (858) 674-2275, ext. 5, or try their website: *www.sdrp.org/sandiegu.htm.*

HISTORY

Indians camped in this area in prehistoric times, finding plenty of the gray-green felsite rock they used to make their tools. There's an old ceremonial site, now closed to the public, where faded pictographs can still be seen.

The reservoir itself was the brainchild of Colonel Ed Fletcher, pioneer water, land, and road developer. In 1911, searching for a steady water source for his coastal developments, he made his way inland on foot from Rancho San Dieguito, following the riverbed until he found the ideal spot for a dam.

Financed by the "land improvement" branch of the Santa Fe Railroad, the dam was completed in 1918 and named for W. E. Hodges, vice-president of the railroad. Bought by the city of San Diego in 1925, the lake was opened for fishing shortly after.

The San Dieguito River Park was created in 1989 when the San Dieguito River Park Joint Powers Authority was formed by the County of San Diego, and the cities of Del Mar, Escondido, Poway, San Diego, and Solana Beach. The aim is "to provide a . . . system of preserved lands with a connecting corridor of walking, equestrian and bicycle trails . . . from the ocean to the river's source."

Walk 1—North Shore Lake View Trail
Distance: 5 miles round trip. *Time:* 2 hours.

A favorite of local joggers and bike riders, this wide road offers fine views of Lake Hodges and the surrounding hillsides. Start at the east end of the parking lot and head for the hills of Rancho Bernardo, walking through meadows of buckwheat, sparsely dotted with laurel sumac. It's quite pretty here in spring, when yellow bushy beardstongue, red monkey flower, and blue and white ceanothus are at their best. In summer, you'll see flashes of yellow tarweed, fennel, and prickly pear cactus flowers, and the long-stemmed red blossoms of chalk-leaf dudleya. If you touch one of the leaves of this succulent, a white chalky powder will come off on your fingers, and you'll see how the plant gets its name. All species of dudleya are named for William Russel Dudley, head of the Botany Department at Stanford University around the turn of the century, and forestry editor of the Sierra Club's magazine.

There are usually a few snowy egrets or great blue herons down by the water, where the shore is lined with willows. In early morning or late afternoon, you may see a raccoon, coyote, or mule deer, or a family of quail skittering across the hillsides. This is snake country, too; keep an eye out for the yellow-banded black king snake, the slim, pink rosy boa, or the less approachable rattlesnake.

The large patches of coast prickly pear are home to a coastal subspecies of cactus wren which, unlike most birds that use their nests only when breeding, live in their nests all year long. As you walk by, listen for their throaty *cha-cha-cha-cha* call.

At about 2 miles, take the path down toward the lakeshore, through a stand of shady oaks. Just below, amidst the mixed greenery, you'll discover pretty little Felicita Creek, burbling cheerfully down from Felicita Park in Escondido (see the next chapter). There are several good spots for creekside picnics here—but be sure to check first for poison oak.

If you want to go on, cross the creek and follow the trail another 2.5 miles to the parking area off Sunset Drive, where the proposed Mule Hill Historical Trail will begin. Call (858) 674-2270 for the latest information.

Walk 2—North Shore Windsurfer Walk
Distance: 3 miles round trip. *Time:* 1 to 1.5 hours.

Start beyond the gate at the Coast-to-Crest sign. This is a favorite drive-in road for windsurfers who love the offshore breezes here, but you can walk in even when the gate is closed—our suggestion.

Lemonade berry, laurel sumac, and toyon line the dusty trail where, if you look closely, you should see animal tracks. Coyotes, snakes, and raccoons are the usual culprits.

Take advantage of shade where you find it. There's a small oak grove about halfway along the trail.

At about 1.5 miles, take the left fork down to the water and the windsurfing area. You can picnic at the water's edge, rent a kayak, or try a little birding. Look for swan-necked Western grebes in the water and turkey vultures overhead, flying like tipsy hawks. They're a lot more impressive on the ground, if you catch them hunched over a meal and get a good view of their bald heads, long red faces, and pale bills.

Someday you'll be able to walk all the way to the dam. For now, continue on through the launching area and uphill to the road before circling back to the lot.

Walk 3—South Shore Bernardo Bay Loop
Distance: 1.5 miles round trip. *Time:* 1 to 1.5 hours.

Walk in toward the information kiosk and turn to your left, heading through buckwheat and broom toward the lake. In 1999, Lake Hodges was declared a globally important bird area. With more than 200 species, some of the best birding in the county can be found on this section of trail. On our last visit here, we saw two pairs of California gnatcatchers, a great-tailed grackle, and a pair of roadrunners in our first 0.2 mile! This is a gnatcatcher paradise, with 80 pairs of the tiny endangered birds nesting here. Grackles, too, like the territory. A few years ago, they could only be seen on the Arizona side of the Colorado River. Now, like so many other species, they've settled in near the lake.

Stay close to the shore, keeping the lake on your left and heading for the hills. Take any of the small fishermen's paths to the water's edge, and study the birds. This is a good spot for grebe-watching. In spring, if you're

Lake Hodges

lucky, you'll see their courtship display, where the mating pair run on wa-ter, side by side, for 20 feet or more. Later in the season, look for fluffy ba-bies, sometimes catching a ride on mama's back. You can also see mallards in eclipse plumage, when the green-headed males take on a somewhat spicier version of the dull brown coloration of their mates. This gender cam-ouflage, along with the loss of their primary flight feathers, turns these oth-erwise flighty fathers into stay-at-home dads till the ducklings are ready to fly off on their own.

There are tules down by the lake, California's version of the bulrushes baby Moses was found in. Notice the triangular shape of their stalks. There's an old saying: "Sedges have edges and rushes are round." Though called bulrushes, tules are obvious sedges.

Follow along the lake, admiring the views nicely fringed by mulefat and willows. The trail narrows and ascends, veering off to the right in the direc-tion of a small oak grove. This is a good place for a shade break or lunch. From here, you can see tiny hikers or bikers across the lake on Walk 1.

When you're ready to move on, take the wooden steps downhill and continue through the buckwheat and sages, turning right at the horehound—a sage relative—and passing a pleasant cove before moving into the willows. Where the trail forks, head uphill toward the sycamores. Bear left along the wide-open trail and stay on it till you come to a Y-intersection, then bear right. You'll see the kiosk and the parking lot just ahead.

Walk 4—South Shore Piedras Pintadas Trail
Distance: 2.5 miles round trip. *Time:* 1 to 1.5 hours.

You can take the longer, 3.8-mile version of this walk by starting at the same place as for Walk 3, and following the signs. Our way is shorter, more suburban, but still very nice.

Follow the white fence in past the sycamores and other pretty plantings; there's wilder growth in the creek bed to your right. Not long ago, this was the middle of nowhere. We're not crazy about all the development, but we do appreciate the shade.

After you pass the last of the houses, take the first path that forks to your right, under the powerlines, and head for the waterfall overlook. These days, you can't go down to the little waterfall, or up to the painted rocks for which this trail is named. After much vandalism, the site is off limits to visitors. Piedras Pintadas may have been the site of young Kumeyaay girls' coming-of-age rites. If you have strong binoculars, you should be able to see the faded red maze designs painted with iron oxide 500 years ago.

With your naked eyes, you can see a comparison of San Diego's two basic bedrocks. In the distance, to your right, look for Hill 498, named for its height, topped with jagged volcanic rocks. Around the waterfall are younger granite boulders, part of the Southern California batholith that stretches from Riverside County to Baja California.

After the waterfall, go back to the main path and follow the wood fencing uphill to the signed nature trail. It's a pleasant loop with good views and lovely spring flowers. As you head back, the labeled grinding holes you pass are fake ones, designed to give an idea of what they look like while protecting the real ones downstream. If you're not ready to loop back right away, you can continue westward along the lakeshore, as far as the rock promontory at Fletcher Point.

Highland Valley Trail

LOCATION
Rancho Bernardo (TG1150:B5). Park in the small lot at the corner of Highland Valley Road and Pomerado Road across from the Pepper Tree Nursery.

DESCRIPTION
Overlooking Lake Hodges from a distance but still part of San Dieguito River Park is this 2-mile hillside trail through the San Pasqual Agricultural Preserve. Though it's mostly an open path through sagebrush and sages, you can still find an oak-shaded creekside spot to picnic. In springtime, look

for the yellow violets called Johnny-jump-ups and the aptly named Chinese houses, small magenta and lavender flowers with a definite pagoda shape. The buzzy trill you may hear is the sound of a Bewick's wren, a small tan-breasted bird with white eyeline. Its name (pronounced Buick) was given by Audubon to honor a fellow artist/ornithologist, the Englishman Thomas Bewick, who illustrated a *History of British Birds* in 1787.

16 FELICITA PARK

LOCATION
Escondido. Take I-15 to Via Rancho Parkway. Go west 1 mile to Felicita Road, turn right, then left into the park(TG1149:J1).

HOURS
9:30 A.M. to sunset. Parking fee.

DESCRIPTION
With 53 acres of rolling hills, shade trees, and flat grassy areas, split by a pleasant year-round creek, this pretty county park offers family and group picnicking, playgrounds, horseshoe pits, and covered dance pavilions. The ranger will open the tiny museum, with its Indian artifacts and historical

photos, for interested groups. There are two nature trails, the Ipai Trail and the North Creek Nature Trail; ask at the ranger office for printed trail guides. For group reservations, call County Parks, (858) 694-3049.

HISTORY

For hundreds of years, Felicita was the site of an Ipai village. It had all the features the Indians prized: a reliable water source, a good supply of acorns, and convenient granite rocks on which to grind them.

Felicita was the name of a chief's daughter who nursed a wounded American soldier back to health after the Battle of San Pasqual. An annual pageant, something like the Ramona Pageant, used to be performed in her honor.

The Walk

Distance: 1.5 miles round trip. *Time:* 45 minutes.

Since the two nature trails are short, we like to combine them into one satisfying double loop.

Park in the first lot at Area 6, and walk back to the stop sign, crossing the main road that leads to the upper parking area. Pick up the Ipai Trail to the left of the creek.

Besides live oaks, there are fan palms, sycamores, and lacy-leafed pepper trees along the trail. The palms were originally "planted" by birds and coyotes that ate the fruits whole and left the pits behind in their droppings, giving the seeds some instant fertilizer.

Look for gopher holes on the trail, and all over the park. They're covered with mounds of freshly dug dirt, which is how you can tell them from the uncovered holes of ground squirrels. Hawks and owls keep an eye on both kinds of holes, watching for a meal.

At about 0.25 mile, you'll see some of the granite boulders typical of the area. Continue around them to the path that leads down to the shallow creek. It's easy to cross without getting your feet wet; just look for a likely spot.

On the other side, heading back along the creek, stop near marker #4 to admire the little waterfalls. On a quiet morning, you might find a hawk or a raven taking a bath. Notice the bowl-shaped grinding holes in the gray rocks where, for centuries, Ipai women went through the tedious business of turning acorns into flour—drying, shelling, pounding, sifting, and pounding some more. The bitter tannic acid had to be leached out with water before the flour could be cooked into mush. The whole process could take days, but grinding was a social affair, a good time to catch up on the latest gossip.

Waterfall at Felicita Park

Leaving the grinding holes, follow the rock-lined path uphill to #1, and the trail's actual beginning. (Yes, we've taken you backwards again.) From here, cross the parking lot to the "WALK—PARK OFFICE" sign. Take the steps up toward the ranger's office, then the gravel path past the cactus garden and down toward the first parking lot. Walk left along the creek to the second small bridge, close to the restrooms, at about 0.9 mile, and cross. After wet weather, you can find dozens of odd-looking mushrooms growing under the live oaks—look, but don't taste.

The gravel path leads to a third bridge across the creek and the start of the self-guiding North Creek Nature Trail. As you head uphill, past arroyo willows and other streamside vegetation, notice how fallen trees and stumps have sprouted new life from their dead trunks. In early spring, if you look carefully, you'll find a few tiny ferns, but it's easier to spot the wild cucumber vine, with its large green leaves and small white flowers, twining its curly tendrils over everything. By summer, the vines are dry and stringy, almost invisible.

A few hundred yards in from the trailhead is a wildlife observation area where a convenient bench faces several nesting boxes and bird feeders set in the trees. Ash-throated flycatchers, bluebirds, woodpeckers, and house wrens may be seen here in spring, and it's always a good spot for a quiet moment.

Down by the creek, look for water striders cruising along in search of food. The feet of these insects have water-repellent hairs that allow them to skim the surface so they are actually walking on water.

Leaving the creek side and heading uphill, you'll pass more grinding holes. With the help of the information plaques, stop and compare the Engelmann oak with its neighboring coast live oak. Both are live oaks—that is, they don't lose their leaves in winter—but the Engelmann's leaf is larger and more oval, while the coast live oak has small, notched, cupped leaves. Coast live oaks have slim acorns; Engelmann acorns are round and fat.

From here, we move into an open section of buckwheat, chamise, and sage. In season, there's a beautiful assortment of wildflowers here; the wine-red peonies are particularly striking in early spring.

At 1.4 miles, pick up the paved path heading down to Area 6, and, per-haps, a nice post-walk picnic. Take a look at the big sycamore beside the toddlers' playground; its soft wood is full of woodpecker storage holes. Starlings, house wrens, and woodpeckers all use this tree for their hollowed-out nests. Barn owls like to perch in the branches; on the ground below, you can often find owl pellets containing tiny gopher skulls and bones.

17 LAKE POWAY

LOCATION

Poway. From I-15, take Rancho Bernardo Road east. After crossing Pomerado, Rancho Bernardo becomes Espola. Continue on Espola to Lake Poway Road. Turn left and drive to the entrance booth (TG1170:H4).

HOURS

Park open daily, 7:00 A.M. to sunset. Lake, Wednesday through Sunday, 7:00 A.M. to sunset. Parking is free to Poway residents. Others pay $4.00 on weekends, April through October.

DESCRIPTION

This fine lake (man-made, of course) and its surrounding wilderness area are good news for walkers, part of the city of Poway's system of hiking and

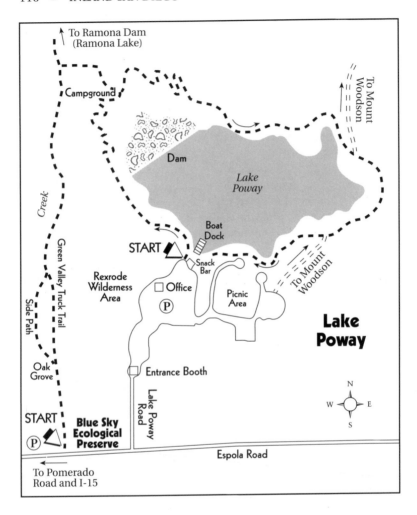

To Ramona Dam
(Ramona Lake)

To Mount Woodson

Campground

Creek

Green Valley Truck Trail

Side Path

Dam

Lake Poway

Boat Dock

START

Snack Bar

Rexrode Wilderness Area

Office

P

Picnic Area

To Mount Woodson

Lake Poway

Oak Grove

Entrance Booth

N
W — E
S

START

P

Blue Sky Ecological Preserve

Lake Poway Road

Espola Road

To Pomerado Road and I-15

equestrian trails that connect residential neighborhoods with parks and open spaces. Daily fishing permits and state licenses may be purchased at the lake concession. You can rent a boat here or launch your own.

There's a walk-in campground near the lake's northwest corner, and a dock and equestrian staging area to the south. There are also playgrounds, volleyball courts, horseshoe pits, a softball field, and nice grassy areas for picnicking. It can get hot out here in summer, and cold in winter. If you plan on walking, dress accordingly. In summer, carry drinking water. For more information, call (858) 679-4393.

HISTORY

Poway, incorporated as a city in 1980, took its name from an old Indian word which seems to have meant "meeting place of the valleys." Since there were year-round streams, cattle from the San Diego Mission were grazed here. The dam was completed in 1971, creating the 60-acre lake.

The 405 acres of undeveloped land around Lake Poway are named in honor of Clyde E. Rexrode, first mayor of Poway, who devoted himself to preserving its open spaces.

The Walk
Distance: 3.2 miles round trip. *Time:* 2 to 2.5 hours.

Look for the trail to the left of the concession. If walking isn't your only interest, you can stroll out on the floating dock and fish-watch, or rent a boat, or feed the ducks. You might just want to sit down on a bench along the first short stretch of trail and survey the lake before you start hiking; we did.

The broad trail soon narrows. The rock triangle you see in the notch between the mountains to the north is the Ramona Dam, built in 1988. The narrow stone strip in the foreground is Poway Dam, which is fenced off. The trail we are following, the Warren Canyon Trail, goes around the base of Poway Dam, which is as close as you can get.

A sign will inform you that you're entering the Rexrode Wilderness Area. Don't be put off by the steep beginning; just take it easy and enjoy the view.

Bear right at #1 on the old nature trail, heading into the ever-popular sage scrub. Look for turkey vultures flying over the water. From the distance, they look like large, dark hawks, but they don't glide as smoothly, and their wings are more V-shaped.

Keep bearing right, and follow the signs toward the walk-in campground. Watch your step on the downhill—a walking stick is helpful here if you're not very sure of foot. Stick to the main trail, ignoring the offshoots; in late spring, look for fleabane, a small yellow-centered lavender daisy, thought to be a natural flea repellent. It must work, because the last time we were here, we didn't see a single flea, though we were bitten by almost every other insect known to man as we made our way down to the foot of the dam. In the small buggy creek where willows, cattails, and poison oak grow, look for Hooker's evening primrose in spring and summer. These showy yellow flowers are named for the nineteenth-century botanist who was director of the Royal Botanical Gardens at Kew, near London.

At #4, there's a watering trough, which sometimes doubles as a bird-bath. The trail continues downhill. At about a mile, there's a fork in the

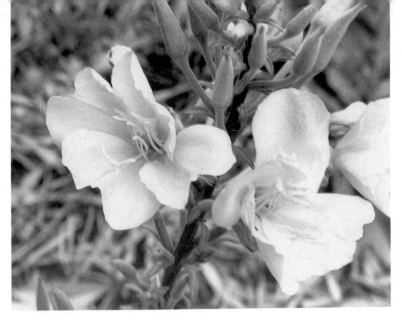

Hooker's Evening Primrose (Photo by Barbara Moore)

road; we like to go left down the steep road to the shady campground for a picnic break or a drink of water. There are restrooms, tables, and barbecues but rarely any people here, and you can admire the live oaks and sycamores, and the lone pine by the side of the babbling but mostly invisible brook. From here, you can squeeze through the fence to continue into Blue Sky Ecological Preserve (see below).

Back on the road again, go up to the fork and start heading left up and around the lake. It really feels like a wilderness here, as you tramp past rocky boulders under a serene blue sky, heading away from the dam. At about 1.5 miles, you start heading toward it again, climbing all the way; the views into the distant hazy mountains are a kind of compensation.

About 2 miles from the trailhead, you come to the top of the dam and start seeing the lake again. A bit farther on, you emerge from the Warren Canyon Trail and start left around the lake, back on the wide trail.

At Pine Point, another nice spot to consider for a picnic, you'll see the first portapotties. On the hillsides above the second pair of portapotties—well, not all the trail's features are scenic—you should see blue ceanothus and red heart-leaf penstemon, if you're here in the spring. As you start uphill again, you'll get a good view of the small coves of Pine Point.

Bear left at the top of the hill and take the lower and wider of the two trails going past the information kiosk. The milepost says 1 mile to the end of the trail; you can make it. Again, there's a bit of a climb, but after the half-mile marker, it's downhill all the way, bearing right and heading toward the grassy area by the boat dock.

If you haven't picnicked yet, consider stopping here. If you're not tired, the trailhead to Mount Woodson is near the equestrian staging area. It's a more strenuous undertaking—but don't let us stop you.

Blue Sky Ecological Preserve

LOCATION
Poway. From I-15, take Rancho Bernardo Road east. Rancho Bernardo becomes Espola Road. Just after the road curves right, you'll find the Blue Sky parking area on your left (TG1170:G3).

DESCRIPTION
Saved from development in 1991, the Blue Sky Ecological Preserve is a great place to hike, bike, picnic, or ride your pony, with a trail that leads into the Lake Poway loop described above. Guided nature walks are offered on weekends; call (858) 679-5469 for information. The sky really does seem bluer here, and spring flowers are especially colorful. Look for blue lupines, pink onions, orange monkey-flower, and magenta chaparral pea.

Walk in on the wide Green Valley Truck Trail. At the first fork, take the road less traveled—a marked path through a large, lovely oak grove where only walkers can go. After rejoining the main road, turn right at the Lake Poway sign, about a mile from the trailhead. If you stay on the road, you'll pass the outdoor classroom area, a good spot to picnic. Ahead, a marked trail to the left leads to Ramona Lake, 1.4 miles away. Don't be fooled by the shady beginning; this trail's hot and steep. Carry water, and don't pick a midsummer day.

We usually head for the peaceful walk-in campground, even better for picnics, with restrooms, water, and plenty of oak-shaded tables. From here, you can walk uphill about 0.2 mile for a view of two dams—Poway up ahead and Ramona behind you. Follow the switchbacks another 0.5 mile to a scenic overlook, keeping the lake to your left. If you still feel ambitious, you can circle Lake Poway, or rent a boat just downhill at the concession (see the Lake Poway walk).

18 DOS PICOS PARK

LOCATION
Ramona. Take Highway 67 north to Mussey Grade Road, then go south 1 mile to Dos Picos Park Road, which ends at the park entrance (TG1171:H5).

HOURS
9:30 A.M. to sunset. Parking fee.

DESCRIPTION
A backcountry county park with shady live oak trees and a pleasant campground, Dos Picos is a popular place for group picnics. A small stream-fed lake attracts wild and domestic water birds, and many other species frequent the 78 acres of woodlands and chaparral. There are playgrounds, horseshoe pits, and an exercise course, in addition to ample facilities for picnics and barbecues. There's also a tiny but interesting collection of butterflies, skulls, and dried flora at the ranger station near the campground entrance. For information and reservations, call County Parks, (858) 694-3049.

HISTORY
Named for the two mountain peaks most easily seen if you're driving down from Julian, Dos Picos was inhabited by Ipai hundreds of years ago. In 1961, the county acquired the property for a park; originally, it was to be given an Ipai name, but somehow, as in history, the Spanish prevailed.

The Walk
Distance: 2 miles round trip. *Time:* 1 hour.

Unless you're camping, you'll have to park at the picnic area and pick up the nature trail behind the campground. Start at the little wooden bridge at the southeast corner of the lot and head for the maniacal squawking of geese; when you hear them, you'll know why some people use them instead of guard dogs. Take a little detour to the pond to feed the birds or inspect the water for tadpoles; otherwise, take the dirt road heading west toward the campground, following the exercise course, passing a log jungle gym and slides. Watch out for red ants here and elsewhere on the trail; they can crawl up bare legs and bite!

With all the oak trees around, you should see some black-and-white acorn woodpeckers. There's a large and varied bird population in the park, so keep your eyes open.

It's about 0.5 mile to the start of the nature trail, between the caravan area and site #48. The trail climbs a bit at first, but soon levels out; in this direction, the walk is mostly downhill.

Watch out for poison oak, and look for round red galls on the scrub oaks. Though they look like apples, they're really a kind of tumor, formed by the plant in response to a small, stingless wasp. The wasp secretes a fluid that triggers formation of the gall, which serves as food and protection for its eggs until the larvae are ready to go out into the world. Each of the 2000 American species of gall-making insects has its own specific plant host.

As you walk along, you'll have a number of opportunities to look out at the mountains and wonder which of the peaks might have been the two for which the park was named. Closer at hand, notice the lichens and mosses growing on the north side of the rocks, where it's generally cooler and damper. Lichens are really a combination of two different plants living together in that state of mutual benefit called symbiosis. One of them, a type of blue-green algae, converts sunlight into food through photosynthesis. The other, a fungus, shelters the algae and keeps it from drying out.

You'll see plenty of the ubiquitous buckwheat, its flower clusters pink and white in spring, rust-colored in fall. At #9, there's an example of mountain mahogany, an unlikely-looking member of the rose family. It has dark, wedge-shaped leaves, and is most noticeable in late summer and fall, when it's covered with slim, curling white feathers that extend from its seeds.

Number 10 is yerba santa, the "bandaid bush." Indians used its soft gray leaves to cover wounds and staunch the flow of blood. At #11, in spring, you'll see ceanothus—wild lilac—in bloom. The white variety is fairly unremarkable, but the blue does resemble miniature lilacs.

Just beyond, looking westward, the stone wall you see is the back side of the reservoir. You can start at its northern end and walk through the spillway, whose well-made walls and stone steps seem a rather ambitious project for such a small body of water. In a few minutes, you'll be passing the pond again, just a goose-honk away from the parking lot.

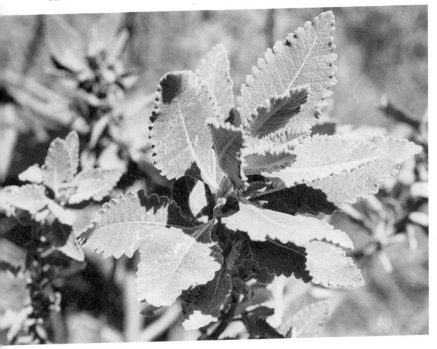

Yerba Santa

Note: On Highway 67, near town, you can buy fresh eggs, game meats, produce, and plants. Ramona, named for the heroine of Helen Hunt Jackson's romantic novel, has an interesting relationship with animals. It used to be the turkey capital of the West and once had a llama as honorary mayor.

19 LAKE SUTHERLAND

LOCATION
Ramona. Take I-8 east to Highway 67. Go north to Ramona and take Highway 78 east to Sutherland Dam Road, which leads to the lake entrance. Drive down toward the boat dock and park in the upper lot just below the concession (TG409:H11).

HOURS
Sunrise to sunset, Friday through Sunday, March through mid-October (subject to change).

DESCRIPTION

A beautiful and relatively unvisited city reservoir, Lake Sutherland is ringed by Indian reservations, an agricultural preserve, and the Cleveland National Forest. It offers good fishing, a small, tree-shaded picnic area, snack bar/concession, boat launch, and a dock where rental boats are available. At present, there are portapotties scattered around the lake and restrooms near the concession.

This is a good place to look for wildlife—eagles, osprey, deer, and even bobcats are not uncommon. For more information, and to confirm hours, call (760) 788-2058.

HISTORY

Centuries ago, the area around Santa Ysabel Creek, Lake Sutherland's main water source, was inhabited by Indians; there are grinding holes in the rock outcroppings not far from the dock.

The dam was begun in 1929, but financial and political problems postponed its completion until 1953, when the lake was opened to the public for fishing.

Water levels here can fluctuate dramatically. In 1978, 46 inches of rain

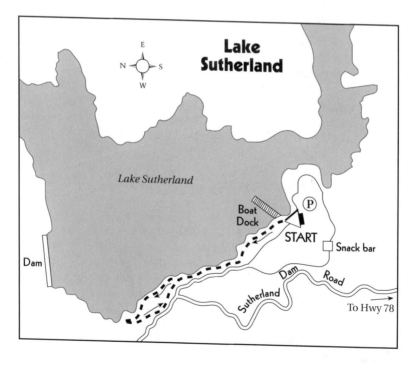

overfilled the dam. In 1988, the reservoir contained 10 percent of its normal volume. In 1998, it was full again.

The Walk
Distance: 2 miles round trip. *Time:* 1 hour.

From the parking lot, take the upper dirt road north alongside the live oaks until it forks after 100 feet or so, heading toward the dam.

In spring, the hillsides here are covered with mustard and blue ceanothus. In summer, there's telegraph weed in bloom. The tall stalks topped with small yellow flowers are a sure sign of a disturbed area, once used for grazing cattle.

Year-round, look for the resident golden eagle flying overhead; it likes to perch in the dead trees on either side of the boat dock. You may also see an occasional osprey, or the distinctive profile of a kingfisher, a small bird with a big crested head.

In the water, you can usually see a great blue heron or two; ducks and geese come by in late fall, and so do duck hunters. While you're watching for birds, stay out of the deposits of illegally grazing cows, which are supposed to be restricted to the east side of the lake.

At about 0.8 mile, you can follow the trail down to a little green island, revealed only in times of low water; there are some Indian grinding holes here too. If the water's too high, or you're not in the mood, continue on about another 0.1 mile till you come to a crossroads.

Here, take the right-forking path toward the dam, which looks like a wall of seventeen slanting silos and is said to be one of the most earthquake-proof dams around. Built on a 45-degree angle, it's even more fascinating seen from behind. If you're a dam fan, special group tours can be arranged with the dam keeper.

Bear left at the bottom of the path, continuing on through rows of mulefat. If you smell something pungent, it's epazote, an herb that does wonders for Mexican beans.

The trail fades away, but without much trouble you can make your way down to the water's edge, across usually dry, cracked salt flats that feel as if you're walking on styrofoam. There are some comfortable rocks where you can sit and enjoy the view—if the water's low enough.

If you wish, continue on the road another 0.25 mile for a closer look at the dam. You can go as far as the buoy line; after that, access is restricted.

Otherwise, go uphill and into the trees, and start circling back. Here, you'll be walking through live oaks, Engelmann oaks, and red-barked manzanita; on a hot day, of which there are many out here, you'll be grateful for the shade.

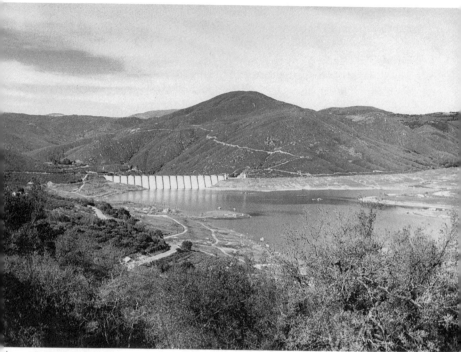

Lake Sutherland

There are fine views down to the lake as you continue uphill for a short way, along the eroded trail that soon joins the paved vehicle road. Then you start downhill, picking up a wide dirt road to your left after about 0.2 mile.

Again, you'll meet the main road, briefly, and again take the dirt road left and back down to the parking lot. Keep an eye out for cars here; this is the main exit road.

You can stop for a drink at the concession stand, or picnic on the hill just behind it—it's time for a break!

20 SYCAMORE CANYON AND GOODAN RANCH

LOCATION
Poway. From I-15, go east on Poway Road to Garden Road. Turn right, go past Garden Park, and turn right on Sycamore Canyon Road. Continue on 2.3 miles to the parking lot. The trailhead is just to the left of the gate by an information kiosk (TG1191:C6).

HOURS
Sunrise to sunset.

DESCRIPTION
These joined open-space preserves, totaling 2025 acres, offer long and short walks through chaparral-covered hills and canyons, impressive views, shady groves, and all sorts of wildflowers. The trail is the first part of a planned system of hiking/equestrian trails from Poway to Santee. Someday there will be trails running all through the valley, connecting into Santee Lakes and Mission Trails Regional Park. It can get hot out here, especially in summer, so dress accordingly and carry water. To date, there are no facilities.

HISTORY
Centuries ago, this area, with its then year-round water source and steady supply of live oak acorns, was an Indian campsite. In the late 1800s, a group of German farmers settled here and founded the tiny town of Stowe. Fifteen families grew oats, wheat, and other crops, and built their own school

and post office, of which not a trace remains. The town died in 1906, when the families went their separate ways. The 325-acre Goodan Ranch was a working ranch in the 1930s, and raised alfalfa to feed the horses at the Del Mar Racetrack. Slated for development, it was jointly purchased in 1991 by the state, county, and the cities of Poway and Santee. The old ranch house, water tower, and windmill are still in use.

The Walk
Distance: 4 miles round trip. *Time:* 1.5 to 2 hours.

Start at the information kiosk, with its good-sized map of the area, and take the trail uphill. In spring, the hillsides are covered with the yellow of sunflowers, rock rose, golden yarrow, and the tall shrubs called bushy beardstongue. There's lots of blue ceanothus too; the flowers of this inland variety are much bluer than those near the coast. The buckwheat here grows like trees; this is full-scale chaparral, not the softer, lower-growing coastal sage scrub.

The path climbs steadily but gently, offering good views of Goodan Ranch. The pale green ground cover whose white flowers look like hundreds of tiny eyes is rattlesnake weed, also known as squaw purge or golandrina, which means "swallow." It's said to cure rattlesnake bites—but don't count on it!

At 0.1 mile, near the top of the first rise, step up on the large flat rock, and see if you can see, in the notch of the distant mountains, a silver sliver of Santee Lakes. Cowles Mountain is the tallest peak to the left, with a little antenna on top. Next highest, to the right, is Fortuna Mountain. Both are part of Mission Trails Regional Park.

After the rise comes a downhill stretch. Then the path undulates up and down, changing your point of view on the surrounding scenery.

At about a mile, there's a pleasant oak-shaded spot with a dry creek bed that will start flowing after winter rains. This would be a good place for a picnic; or, even better, try the larger grove about 0.5 mile farther on, the Martha Harville Memorial Grove, named for a young park ranger who helped develop the park and asked that her ashes be scattered here. You'll find benches and, to the left of the trail, some old grinding holes. Look for the bowl-shaped indentations in the rocks where Indian women spent long hours pounding acorns into meal.

Owls roost in these trees. Look on the ground for their pellets, the fur balls they spit out, with the tiny skulls and bones of their rodent dinners still inside. In spring, there are wild roses blooming. Lean over to catch their sweet scent, but stay on the trail and out of the poison oak. The creek

Indian grinding holes

bed here is where the Stowe Post Office is said to have been—not that any-one has managed to find any sign of it.

The woodsy area soon ends, and you're back in the open again. Continue on about a mile to a wide dirt road. Here you can turn right, and then right again at the crossroads to circle back north to the parking lot. We go on, crossing the dirt road and following the marked trail that leads toward the creek. Bear right until you come to an old olive grove that is now a picnic area. Turn right and make your way through the grove until you come to the ranch house.

Notice the windmill and water tower. Before World War II, wind power was a good, cheap way to pump water from local sources like Sycamore Creek. Nowadays, electricity rules, and 90 percent of our water is imported.

Imagine what it might have been like living here in the 1930s, and then take the wide dirt road heading north to your air-conditioned car. Look for lark sparrows feeding along the side of the road. They're easy to spot with their striking rust-and-white masks.

Incidentally, rangers tell us that there are several rare plants growing in these parts: San Diego thornmint, mesa clubmoss, copperleaf, and chocolate lily. We didn't see any of them; maybe you'll do better.

21 ROSE CANYON HIKING PARK

LOCATION
University City. Take I-5 north to La Jolla Village Drive. Go east to Genesee Avenue, then south to Decoro Street, where you can park. Walk south about 0.2 mile along busy Genesee to the park entrance, across from University City High School (TG1228:D4).

HOURS
Sunrise to sunset.

DESCRIPTION
With 275 acres of open space surrounding the old roadbed of the Santa Fe Railroad, Rose Canyon is a pleasant oasis in one of the fastest-growing areas of the city. There are no facilities. For more information, call (858) 581-9952.

HISTORY
In 1769, Gaspar de Portola, military commander of the Sacred Expedition that brought Father Serra to San Diego, rested his men here on their way up north. A hundred years later, the area was named for Louis Rose, a Texan who came to San Diego in 1850, tanned hides in the canyon, acted as Old Town postmaster for ten years, and developed a community called Roseville in what is now the business district of Point Loma.

The Walk
Distance: 3 miles round trip. *Time:* 1 to 1.5 hours.

Follow the broad maintenance trail along Rose Creek, which flows into Mission Bay. Across the creek is the "new" roadbed of the Santa Fe Railroad.

The first wooded section of trail is the nicest. In winter, when the sycamores are bare, you can easily see the large stick nests of hawks and owls. Owls start nesting in February; if you notice a catlike face staring at you from a treetop nest, it's a great horned owl. They usually raise three or four chicks that resemble fuzzy tennis balls when they first hatch. One nest may be used interchangeably, year after year, by owls, hawks, and ravens.

By June, you'll see many immature hawks, bigger than their parents, exercising their wings by flapping and jumping up and down near their nest. Once we saw a pair of red-tails working out so vigorously on the edge of their nest, they actually knocked it out of the tree.

Starting at 0.3 mile on the right is a large patch of nightshade, a tomato relative with gray leaves and pale blue flowers in spring, and tiny round yellow fruits in fall and winter. Also in spring, there's lots of fennel, yellow mustard, and pink thistle, as well as exotic escapees from the hilltop yards.

As you continue into the open area, houses and the railroad tracks come more into view. Despite these intrusions, most of the canyon is pretty quiet, except for the occasional rumble of passing trains.

With all the "Golden Triangle" development just to the north, what's left of the local wildlife has been forced into the canyon. In spring, particularly, watch for rattlesnakes, which seem to like it here.

About 1.5 miles in, you'll reach the remains of an old wooden railroad

Autumn in the sycamores (Photo by Bill Evarts, courtesy of the San Diego Natural History Museum)

bridge, at the foot of the powerlines. From here on, the sounds of I-5 traffic overwhelm the sounds of bird calls—as good a time as any to start heading back.

A Word About Streamsides

San Diego definitely has its ups and downs. Our high tabletop mesas are split by rugged canyons and broad valleys that were carved out by eons of runoff water, creating a complex drainage system of rivers and creeks that flow into the sea.

In the bottoms of these canyons and valleys we find what is called the streamside or riparian (riverbank) plant community. Even where the streams are only seasonal, there is still enough water to support large, thirsty trees like sycamores, coast live oaks, and cottonwoods. All plants drink and eliminate water, much as we do, and sycamores are particularly heavy drinkers. A single tree needs 300 gallons a day to survive—that's six bathtubs-full!

San Diego's streamsides are some of its most pleasant locations. Besides the trees, there are tall leafy shrubs like arroyo (creek) willows and mulefat, and water-loving plants like wild roses, California fuchsia, and, less welcome, but undeniably pretty in autumn, poison oak. Foxes, bobcats, deer, raccoons, and many smaller animals and reptiles find these areas good places to live, with plenty of water, food, and shelter. In spring, resident hawks, owls, and woodpeckers share the trees with colorful migrants like orioles, flycatchers, and tanagers.

Indians, too, found streamsides attractive. They liked to set up their camps near water, gather acorns from the live oaks, and use convenient granite boulders for acorn grinding. Centuries of patient pounding hollowed out bowl-like depressions in the granite, sure signs of Indian presence.

In their natural state, streamside communities change slowly, but increasing development of our mesa tops has created new problems—erosion from overwatering; introduced exotic plants like pampas grass, acacia, and thistle, that spread quickly and threaten the survival of natives; and neighborhood cats and dogs that prey on wildlife.

Today, major highways arc over the streamside canyons, or cut right through them. Since they are the lowest places in the county, storm sewers have been installed beneath them, the telltale manholes showing at intervals along the jeep roads built to maintain them. An ignominious fate, perhaps, for our streamsides, but these are the paths we walkers usually follow.

22 SAN CLEMENTE CANYON

LOCATION
University City. From Highway 52, between I-5 and I-805, take Regents Road/Clairemont Mesa Boulevard south to the park entrance, circling right under the Clairemont Mesa overpass to the east parking lot (TG1228:C7). To shorten the walk somewhat, use the alternate entrance at Highway 52 and Genesee Avenue (TG1228:E6).

HOURS
Sunrise to sunset.

DESCRIPTION
Bounded by freeways, San Clemente Canyon has more than 400 wooded acres to explore. There are picnic tables, barbecues, and restrooms near the Clairemont Mesa entrance, restrooms near the Genesee entrance, and benches scattered along the trail. There's an excellent information kiosk near the trailhead, with pictures of flora and fauna you may see on the trail. If there's been any significant rain, try another canyon; too much water can make crisscrossing San Clemente Creek more of a wade than a walk. In fact, you might not even be able to drive into the parking lot. For more information, call (858) 581-9952.

HISTORY
Legend has it that San Clemente Canyon was originally named Cañada Clemente or "Clemente's Glen," after the Indian caretaker of the vineyards, orchards, and gardens planted here by the padres. Somehow, over the years, the canyon, if not Clemente himself, was canonized. Today, San Clemente's official name, Marian Bear Memorial Park, honors the woman

who persuaded Caltrans (the California Department of Transportation) and the city to build Highway 52 on the canyon's higher, drier south side, saving most of its coast live oaks and sycamores from destruction.

The Walk

Distance: 6 miles round trip. *Time:* 2 to 2.5 hours.

Park in the east parking lot and follow the broad dirt vehicle road heading east. On your left, in the creek bed, are tall old sycamores, shorter arroyo willows, and mulefat, once a prime food source for mules and cattle. Some of the finest sycamores in town are in this canyon—green in spring, gold in autumn, white skeletons in winter. Keep an eye out for poison oak, which twines in vast quantities around the sycamores. One of us managed to get a rash from just brushing up against some dried winter twigs, so watch where you swing your arms.

As you walk along, notice the cockleburs. They stick to anything they touch—dogs, clothes, each other—and are said to have inspired the invention of Velcro. Cockleburs use their stick-to-itiveness to spread their seeds. Taking no chances, they have a natural seed bank, with two kinds of seeds—one for this year and one for next—in case there's not enough rain to start the first batch growing.

There's a lot of horehound here too. A non-native member of the mint family, it has leaves like a geranium and flowers like a sage, stems of white clusters that turn to brown seed pods in fall. Europeans brought horehound to America, and Americans brought it to California to use as a cold remedy. Horehound candies were the cough drops of yesteryear, though a lot of honey had to be added to mask the natural bitterness.

Even though the sounds of traffic never quite disappear, you can still manage to hear the tapping of striped black-and-white Nuttall's woodpeckers busily probing the porous bark of the sycamores for insects. These woodpeckers have long, barbed tongues, good for getting into small crevices to spear their hors d'oeuvres.

Turn right after the half-mile marker, just before the first creek crossing, and take the narrow path uphill and into the live oaks. After a bit, there's a short, steep descent—maybe 6 feet or so—that's a little tricky to negotiate unless your shoes have very good treads. This is a pretty route, but you can stay on the main trail if you prefer.

Continuing eastward, follow the creek through the oak woodlands. In early spring, you'll notice the fuchsia-flowered gooseberry, whose small red flowers look like cultivated fuchsias. They're followed by hairy berries that birds and foxes love to eat. Indians added the berries to meat to make

San Clemente Creek

pemmican, a staple food for long trips and hard times. By June, this thorny bush is leafless; more obvious then are the wild roses, tiny red geraniums, and lavender checkerbloom.

At the next fork in the trail, we like to go left into the live oaks for a shady break. In dry weather, you can walk up the cobblestone creek bed; the cobbles are Mexican immigrants, formed by a volcanic episode that occurred about 45 million years ago, near what is now Guaymas, in Sonora, Mexico. They were carried here by an ancient river with the help of the same continental plate movement that created the Sea of Cortez and the San Andreas Fault. Local Indians found these smooth rounded rocks just the right size to use as pestles for grinding seeds and acorns.

Just past the one-mile marker, cross under the Genesee overpass, taking the path closest to the creek. Look in the small ponds for mosquito fish, planted in spring to keep mosquito larvae under control. You may also see the eggs of freshwater snails on the undersides of leaves floating in the water, and masses of frog eggs on the surface. In late spring, these hatch into tadpoles; the tiny ones become tree frogs, the larger ones, bullfrogs. Up ahead, bear right, heading into the shady oaks.

Some years ago, when San Clemente's storm sewers were upgraded, the canyon floor was dug up and hydro-seeded with a wildflower mix to prevent erosion. Unfortunately, nobody thought to choose seeds of local wildflowers, so most bloomed for a season and died. One of the survivors was common yarrow, with its soft ferny leaves and 3-foot-high flower stalks. Another survivor was fuller's teasel, a somewhat taller thistle-like plant. Fuller is an old word for cloth maker, and the bristly seed pods were used in Europe years ago to card wool. Keep an eye out for both these plants as you walk on.

You can follow the trail all the way to I-805, or stop, as we often do, on a bench within sight of sewer standpipe #185 to admire the wildflowers, the result of a more recent reseeding project.

23 TECOLOTE CANYON NATURAL PARK

LOCATION
Clairemont.

For Walk 1: From I-805, take Clairemont Mesa Boulevard west to Genesee Avenue. Turn left and go one block to Bannock; turn right and park near North Clairemont Park and Recreation Center (TG1248:F1).

For Walk 2: From I-805, take Balboa Avenue west to Genesee Avenue. Go south to Marlesta Drive, opposite Mesa College. Park north of the traffic light and walk 0.25 mile to the park entrance (TG1248:H5).

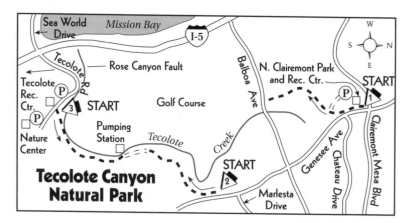

Linda Vista.

For Walk 3: From I-5, take the Sea World Drive exit. Go east on Tecolote Road past the Tecolote Canyon Park and Recreation Center to Tecolote Nature Center (TG1268:F2).

HOURS

Park, sunrise to sunset. Nature Center, 8:00 A.M. to 3:00 P.M. weekends; call (858) 581-9952 for weekday hours.

DESCRIPTION

At more than 900 acres, Tecolote is one of our larger urban canyons. It is unusual because it runs north to south, rather than east to west, as most streamside canyons do. *Tecolote* is a Mexican word for "owl," and there are definitely owls living here, along with hawks and many kinds of songbirds. Keep your eyes open for poison oak, especially in less traveled areas.

There are restrooms, picnic tables and barbecues, ballfields, basketball courts, and a playground at the Tecolote Recreation Center. There are similar facilities at North Clairemont Park.

HISTORY

Tecolote has been on the map for 200 years and shows evidence of 2500 years of Indian residence. Until 1953, cattle were grazed near the mouth of the canyon, which was used as a gravel pit during the building of I-5. In 1957, when the city decided to dump landfill in the canyon and turn the gravel pit into a city operations yard, the first community protests began. They went on for eighteen years, until Tecolote was finally set aside as an open-space park, a victory that led to the preservation of our other urban canyons. Local residents, originally asked to contribute to the purchase of Tecolote, later had their money returned by the city. Many refused the refund, instead using the money to reintroduce native plants into the canyon.

Walk 1—Chateau Drive Trail

Distance: 3.5 miles round trip. *Time:* 1.5 hours.

Whether you approach from the south end of the North Clairemont Park and Recreation Center, descending a steep hill strewn with bits of broken glass, or stroll southward 0.4 mile past the roar of Genesee Avenue traffic, or try to dash across in front of that traffic from Chateau Drive to the park entrance—access to this trail leaves something to be desired.

However you manage to get there, the peaceful feeling of Tecolote's shady creekside glades takes over almost immediately. This is our favorite walk in the canyon.

Live oaks predominate. Notice their holly-notched cupped leaves and, in fall and winter, the slim pointed acorns. As you stroll along, you'll see a number of attempts at erosion and flood control: bark chips on the trail, gabions on the creek bank, rocks laid in feeder creeks to form all-weather crossings for maintenance vehicles.

In late winter, you may be lucky enough to see a pair of kites engaged in their prenuptial flights. Their courtship ritual involves the male passing a dead mouse to his chosen female in midair. Usually, she accepts, they eat together, and then mate. If she turns him down, he'll eat the mouse himself, and try again later.

Gray and white, with black shoulder patches, kites get their name from their habit of "kiting" on the wind, floating down to their prey instead of diving like other hawks.

You can walk all the way south to Balboa Avenue. We turn around a few hundred feet sooner, before the sounds of traffic get a chance to register.

Walk 2—Marlesta Trail
Distance: 2.2 miles round trip. *Time:* 1 hour.

Here again, getting to the trailhead is the only bad part of this trip; you have to walk south alongside the Genesee Avenue traffic. Once you're on the trail, though, you can relax among the live oaks, sycamores, and willows, crossing back and forth over Tecolote Creek.

Coming down from Genesee, take the first creek crossing and then bear right. In fall, look for the red tubular flowers of California fuchsia. Although there's lots of poison oak, you can still find some nice picnic spots among the trees beside the water. The last time we were here, there were more crayfish in the creek than we'd seen in any one location—and that was in the dry season!

At just over a mile, the trail narrows. Ahead is our turnaround, the driving range of the Tecolote Golf Course.

Willow buds

Walk 3—Tecolote Nature Center Trail

Distance: 4 miles round trip. *Time:* 1.5 to 2 hours.

The most suburban of Tecolote's walks also offers the most conveniences, including easy access and ample parking. Surrounded by housing developments and the University of San Diego, this is surely the best known of Tecolote's trails.

Before you begin, stop by the Tecolote Nature Center, whose exhibits and native plant garden are well worth a visit. In spring, the area is bright with yellow chrysanthemums, locally known as "Caltrans daisy" because the seeds were inadvertently spread by the highway department's road-grading equipment. There are a lot of introduced plants in the canyon, including a few century plants with tree-high stalks.

After awhile, the concrete channel gives way to more natural streamside vegetation, the canyon widens, and the houses become less obtrusive. There's a small live oak grove to the left named for canyon activist Marian Bear and, at about 1.5 miles, a recently planted section funded by local residents.

In spring, you'll see golden poppies, California's state flower. Here the creek's flow is interrupted by gabions, stone-filled wire sediment traps—another attempt to control flooding and erosion.

We usually turn around at the gas pumping station just before 2 miles, but you can go all the way to the Marlesta Trail if you want (Walk 2), passing the Tecolote Golf Course up ahead.

BY THE WAY...

Rose Canyon Fault

Back at the Nature Center, you may want to take a quick look at the Rose Canyon Fault, which runs from Mexico into the sea at La Jolla Shores, paralleling the infamous San Andreas Fault part of the way.

Walk westward along the fenced baseball field, then uphill to the upper ballfield. Leaving the pavement where the path forks, follow the fence 20 yards or so, noticing how abruptly the dirt bank on your right changes from cobbles to sandstone. The fault is where the change occurs, separating the 500,000-year-old cobble/dirt conglomerate from the 50-million-year-old Scripps Formation sandstone. Unprepossessing though it may seem, this is one of the few places you can actually see an earthquake fault up close. Most are now covered over by buildings, bushes, and blacktop.

24 SHEPHERD CANYON

LOCATION
Tierrasanta. Take I-15 north to Clairemont Mesa Boulevard. Go east to Santo Road, turn left, and park on Remora Street. Walk back to the sign at the trailhead (TG1249:H1).

HOURS
Sunrise to sunset.

DESCRIPTION
This walking and jogging trail is a surprisingly pretty and peaceful place overlooked by recent development and the playing fields of Tierrasanta Municipal Park. Technically speaking, Shepherd Canyon lies somewhat to the north, but we've never heard this canyon called anything else. There are no facilities.

HISTORY
The area including Shepherd Canyon was once part of Camp Elliott, a 13,000-acre marine training camp used during World War II for artillery and tank training. Unexploded shells may still be found here. Anything suspicious looking should not be touched; it could still be dangerous. It's highly unlikely you'll find any ordnance along the trail, but if you do, mark the location, and call 911 as soon as possible.

The Walk

Distance: 2.5 miles round trip. *Time:* 1 hour.

Arroyo willows and several varieties of eucalyptus line the trail, along with the usual coastal sage scrub. The willows stay green until winter, when they turn golden, providing a sweep of post-fall color. Then they start shedding their leaves, form buds, and go into their spring cycle.

There are several spring wildflowers here that we've rarely found in our other locations. There's enough chaparral broom along the trail to try a little study of plant sex. In autumn, look closely at the broom in bloom. Contrary to what you might expect, the slim, white, hairy flowers are female; the male flowers are rather flat and fuzzy.

At about 0.7 mile, you'll come to a concrete spillway, on the other side of which is a pond where local kids come to practice their casting, hoping to catch one of the five-pound catfish rumored to be hiding here. In spring, you'll see duck and coot mamas leading their babies around the pond. Nearby, look for purple sage, an introduced plant with soft, textured gray leaves and pinkish flowers. In winter, you'll notice the tall stalks of dried seed pod clusters. To the right, in early spring, star lily starts blooming, knee-high stalks of white star-shaped flowers appearing among the tall, grass-like leaves.

Farther uphill, overlooking the pond, keep an eye out for brittlebush, a gray-leafed shrub that looks almost like white sage. It's another introduced plant, more commonly seen in the desert. Related to bush sunflower, it has bright yellow spring flowers.

The trail undulates up and down (mostly up) to a T-intersection. This is our turnaround, though you can continue another 0.1 mile or so to Via Valarta, an alternate point of entry.

Chaparral broom in bloom

25 SAN DIEGO MISSION AND MISSION TRAILS REGIONAL PARK

LOCATION

Mission Gorge.

For Walk 1: Take I-8 east to Mission Gorge Road, then go left under the freeway to Twain Avenue, and left again. Twain Avenue becomes San Diego Mission Road; Mission San Diego de Alcala and its parking lot will be on your right (TG1249:H7).

For Walk 2: Take Mission Gorge Road northeast to Junipero Serra Trail; turn left and park in the Mission Trails Regional Park visitor center lot (TG1250:D2).

For Walk 3: Turn left from the visitor center lot and drive about 1.5 miles to the Mission Dam parking lot on your left (TG1230:F6).

HOURS

San Diego Mission, 9:00 A.M. to 5:00 P.M. Entrance fee.

Mission Trails Regional Park, sunrise to sunset. **Note:** The main vehicle road, Junipero Serra Trail, is closed to traffic from 5:00 P.M. to 8:00 A.M. November 1 to March 31, from 7:00 P.M. to 8:00 A.M. the rest of the year.

DESCRIPTION

A two-stop trip, combining Spanish-era history and a sampling of some of the pleasures of 5800-acre Mission Trails Regional Park, one of the largest urban parks in the country. The Mission San Diego de Alcala—"The Mother of the Missions"—has been restored to a kind of splendor it never really had. Beautifully landscaped, its grounds are a delightful place to spend an hour. Taped tours are available, and guided group tours may be arranged on request; call (619) 283-7319.

Mission Trails Park offers wilder walks through more natural surroundings. The visitor center has excellent exhibits, restrooms, and a gift shop. There are drinking fountains, picnic tables, and portapotties near the dam. Nature walks are offered on Wednesdays, Saturdays, and Sundays, and there is an extensive summer program of special events. Nearby Kumeyaay Lake now offers camping. Call (619) 668-3275 or visit their website *(www.mtrp.org)* for the latest information.

HISTORY

The first of California's twenty-one missions was actually a brushwood shack on Presidio Hill, built under the direction of Father Junipero Serra, shortly after the arrival of the Sacred Expedition of 1769.

To Santee →

San Diego Mission and Mission Trails Regional Park

Oak Canyon Creek

Old Mission Dam

Gate

Trail

START

River

Junipero Serra

San Diego

Gate

Visitor Center

START

Mission Gorge Road

Golfcrest Drive

Jackson Drive

Friars Road

San Diego Mission

START

Twain Avenue

San Diego Mission Road

To I-8 and San Diego River Walk
Presidio Park / Palm Canyon

Moved to this site because of its nearness to the river and its distance from the Spanish soldiers, who couldn't keep their hands off female converts, the rebuilt mission was a second brushwood shack. It was burned and pillaged in 1775 by hundreds of local Indians who didn't appreciate the attempts at their conversion. Father Luis Jayme, killed in the uprising, is buried under the sanctuary. The rebellious Indians sank into the dim mists of history; the Spaniards went on with their conquest.

The mission was rebuilt of less flammable adobe, but its checkered career continued. Damaged by earthquakes, secularized by Mexicans, and later occupied by American soldiers, it was wholly in ruins by the turn of the century. It wasn't till the height of the Depression, when the Spanish period began to take on a rosy glow, that the mission was restored and rededicated. Today, it's a working parish church, as well as a tourist attraction.

The old Mission Dam, built between 1813 and 1816, is a registered national historic monument. It was the first major irrigation project on the West Coast, the start of California agriculture, and the beginning of the end of the unhindered flow of our rivers. The Mission Trails Visitor and Interpretive Center was opened in 1995.

Walk 1—Mission History Stroll
Distance: 0.25 mile. *Time:* 30 minutes.

Admission includes an information brochure and map, and you're welcome to wander through the grounds, admire the gardens, and visit the sanctuary, chapel, and museum. There are informative plaques all over, many of the plants are labeled, and docents in the gift shop are happy to answer any questions you have about mission history.

Inside the church, to the left of the altar, just under the papal umbrella and opposite the small statue of Father Serra, is a dark painting of San Diego de Alcala, said to have been brought here by Serra himself. San Diego, or Saint Didacus (rhymes with Leviticus), was a fifteenth-century Spanish Franciscan. A hundred years after his death, when the son and heir of King Philip II lay dying, he was put to bed with the "incorrupt" body of the old priest and miraculously cured. Philip petitioned Rome on Diego's behalf, and sainthood was granted in 1588, a bad year for the Spanish Armada.

Arriving here on Diego's feast day fourteen years later, Vizcaino renamed the area in honor of his saintly compatriot. Today, despite continuing controversy, Father Serra, too, is well on his way to beatification.

In the small museum are a few relics of San Diego's past, an inexplicable display of New Mexican Indian pottery, and pictures of the mission before its restoration. Outside, in the main quadrangle, are excavations of the old rooms of the monastery, the project of a USD archaeology class in the late 1960s. You can sit under the pepper trees by the fountain and listen to the murmur of the water and the freeway traffic, contemplating the vagaries of history, and the romanticized version of it all around you. Try to envision the surrounding hillsides as they really were a few hundred years ago, all chaparral and silence.

This is a good place to study the birds and the bees. Look for native goldfinches and hummingbirds near the fountain, and imported Mediterranean honeybees buzzing around their hives in the South American pepper trees. Don't forget to walk up the arcade before you leave and look in on the pomegranate, citrus, peach, and loquat trees in the garden of the Virgin of Guadalupe.

Walk 2—Oak Grove/Visitor Center Double Loop

Distance: 2.5 miles round trip. *Time:* 1.5 to 2 hours.

Pick up the Oak Grove Trail on the east side of Junipero Serra, turning right at the information kiosk. The trail heads toward Mission Gorge before looping back into a grove of oaks and willows. There are two kinds of oaks here, coast live oaks and Engelmann oaks. Engelmann was a German expert on cactus who ended up having an oak tree named for him. They're the ones with the large, bluer leaves.

You can sit on a bench or a rock by the creek and enjoy the shade before heading back into the open section of sagebrush, buckwheat, and broom. After 0.5 mile, you'll be back at the main road, Junipero Serra, again.

Cross the road, take a few steps uphill, and you'll be on the Visitor Center Loop. Turn right where the paths converge and keep going. Don't miss the detour down to the Indian grinding holes down by the river; it's the nicest part of the trail. There are large, shady live oaks and even a stone

Old Mission Dam (Photo by Barbara Moore)

throne to sit on. One hot summer morning we saw blue grosbeaks, hummingbirds, phainopeplas, a house wren, a family of swifts, and a Nuttall's woodpecker in one five-minute break. Notice the tree snag across the water that's riddled by woodpecker beaks, and check the water for crayfish and mosquito fish.

Back on the loop, continue toward the cliffs, looking for swifts and cliff swallows swooping toward their nests in the rocks. Swallows pick up bits of river mud for their nests; it takes 1200 pellets to make a single nest. Since swifts never touch ground, they grab whatever nesting material floats by, and stick it together with bird spit—a clever solution to the housing problem.

When the trail comes to a T-intersection, you can, if you're really ambitious and the water level is low enough, cross the river and follow the Suycott Wash Trail up Fortuna Mountain. Or just stop at the water, as we do, before looping back to the visitor center.

Here, deep in the gorge carved out by the once-mighty San Diego River, dammed by the padres in the early 1800s, are remains of the aqueduct that once brought water from the dam to the mission. More recently, this was a "mitigation area," planted with mulefat and willows by the city in return for permission to invade the upstream habitat of the endangered least Bell's vireo during restoration work on Mission Dam. Today, the vegetation is thriving, and if you're lucky you may catch a glimpse of the small, slow-moving, olive-drab vireo, which we hope is thriving too.

Walk 3—Mission Dam/Oak Canyon/Grassland Trail Combo
Distance: 3 miles round trip. *Time:* 1.5 hours.

If you wish, you can start this walk at the visitor center, adding another 3 miles or so to the trip. Whether you walk or drive down Junipero Serra, be sure to scan the cliffs to the east for climbers; this is a popular rock-climbing site.

Old Mission Dam's parking lot is fringed with native trees; take a few minutes to look at their leaf shapes, and you'll never again confuse a cottonwood with a sycamore or a willow. Cottonwood leaves are heart-shaped, and seem to "twinkle" in the wind; sycamores have maple-shaped leaves; and black willow leaves are slim, like knife blades. Don't expect to have much luck with your leaf study in winter, since cottonwoods and the white-barked sycamores are deciduous, and usually bare by December. All these trees are good for birding, especially in the morning and late afternoon. Look for woodpeckers, warblers, and goldfinches.

The dam area has been vastly "improved" since our earliest visits: there are more unshaded picnic tables, a wheelchair-accessible viewing ramp, even audio tape tours are available. Personally, we miss the old days a little, but there's no doubt all the smoothed-out rough edges have attracted more visitors. The Old Mission Dam was designated a historic landmark in 1963. Read the bronze plaque for background before starting out.

The first part of the path is lined with native plantings. Look for wild roses, pink and fragrant in spring, bright with red-orange rose hips (their Vitamin C–rich seed pods) in fall. Cross the wooden bridge that keeps you off the old sewer pipe, which is how we had to get across the river years ago. Follow the path directly in front of you, heading for mulefat, willows, boulders, and the well-marked Oak Canyon Trail. Take advantage of the shady live oaks when you find them; this is largely an open trail, hot in summer, that stays on the high ground alongside Oak Canyon Creek.

In fall, look for red California fuchsia among the buckwheat, broom, and white sage. Live oaks, sycamores, and mulefat line the creek bed, and there are raccoon and deer tracks on the trail, along with the usual coyote "calling card"—grayish, fur-filled droppings.

At the flat rock outcropping a few hundred yards above the creek bed, splotches of chartreuse lichen and green moss can make the rocks look like a painter's dropcloth. If you want, continue up into Oak Canyon and all the way to Highway 52. We usually choose to start back here, retracing our steps till we come to the wooden steps that lead down—and up—to the Mission Dam Viewpoint. Take the short jog right for the view, then follow the Grassland Trail that turns right at the kiosk, crosses the river, and leads to Junipero Serra. Turn right at the road, and you'll soon be back at your car.

While you're in mission history country, here are two urban oases you may want to sample. The first gives you a nice nature break from shopping. The second is easily combined with a visit to the gussied-up historical buildings, boutiques, and restaurants of San Diego's Old Town.

San Diego River Walk

LOCATION
San Diego. Mission Center Road, between Highway 163 and I-805. Park in the small lot at the east end of Hazard Center Drive (TG1269:B2).

DESCRIPTION
A stone's throw from Mission Valley's shopping malls is a wide paved walkway on the banks of the tamed San Diego River, 1.5 miles on each side. Alders, poplars, sycamores, live oaks, elderberry, and black willows block

out the noise of busy highways, and dead trees provide perches for herons, cormorants, and kingfishers. There are always lots of ducks here, and you can usually see brownish moorhens, foraging for food with their candy-corn-colored bills.

Presidio Park and Palm Canyon

LOCATION
Old Town. South of Taylor Street, on Presidio Drive. Park in the small lot below the Presidio building (TG1268:F4).

DESCRIPTION
This pair of grassy municipal parks in the heart of Old San Diego is good for walks, picnics, and historical lore. Presidio Park was the site of California's first Spanish settlement, originally including both the mission and the *presidio* or fortress surrounding it. One of four presidios in California (the others are at Santa Barbara, Monterey, and San Francisco), this one owes its survival to businessman George Marston, who bought the property in the 1920s, calling it the West Coast's Plymouth Rock. He organized the San Diego Historical Society to protect it, hired landscapers to beautify it, covered the ruins to protect them, and donated the park to the

San Diego Presidio

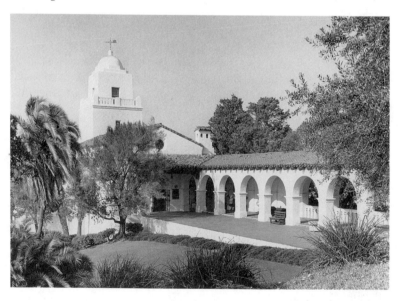

city of San Diego in 1929, a few months before the stock market crash, on the 160th anniversary of Father Serra's arrival. The small Serra Museum, run by the Historical Society, is located here. It's open Tuesday through Sunday in summer, Friday through Sunday in winter. Admission is $5. Call (619) 297-3258 for more information.

Start the walk across from the parking lot, to the right of the area where many Presidio-era artifacts have been unearthed by SDSU archaeology students. As the path heads downhill, curving southward, the roar of the freeway begins to fade. Continue down to the canyon, unless it's winter, a good time to detour to the broad stretch of lawn to your right. Across the road, you'll see a row of tall pine trees, with picnic tables beneath them. From November to March, hundreds of monarch butterflies often come here to roost.

Once you get down to Palm Canyon, cross the wooden bridge and follow the trail uphill, passing a pair of palm-shaded picnic tables and a small parking lot.

Above the lot is a grassy hillside. At the top, just below the houses, look for the birdbath commemorating the White Deer of Mission Hills, an escapee from a small petting zoo across the freeway who briefly made his home in the park. Around the birdbath are animal and bird tracks, immortalized in concrete. A plaque reads: "Bliss in solitude beneath this tree. Formless, silent, spirit free—A friend."

26 LAKE JENNINGS

LOCATION
Lakeside. Take I-8 east to Lake Jennings Park Road; turn left, then right onto Harritt Road. Where Harritt Road divides, go right to the south entrance. Drive in about 2.2 miles along the lake's main road and park where the pavement ends (TG1232:F3).

HOURS
South gate, sunrise to sunset, Friday through Sunday. Night hours in summer. Campground, open to walkers on weekdays, 9:30 A.M. to sunset, 9:30 A.M. to 9:30 P.M. on weekends. Closed September and October.

DESCRIPTION
Lake Jennings is an attractive mountain-ringed reservoir with a 100-acre campground at its northwest corner, and a boat pier, launch ramp, and concession to the south. Popular with fishermen, the lake is operated by the Helix Water District; a day permit and state license are required if you want to try your luck with trout, bass, and catfish. Rowboats and

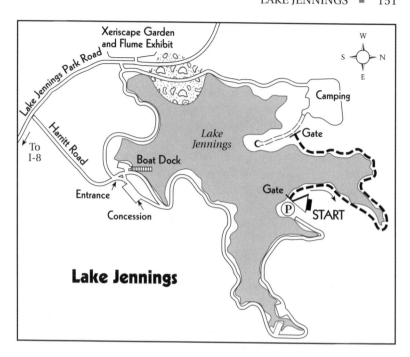

Lake Jennings

electric motorboats can be rented at the pier, or you can launch your own for a small fee. At present, there are no picnic facilities, but some are planned for the future. For camping reservations, call County Parks, (858) 694-3049.

HISTORY

Once part of the 49,000-acre El Cajon Rancho, Lake Jennings, like most of the county's lakes, is a man-made reservoir. The dam was built in 1962 by the Helix Irrigation District, and named for its first general manager, Chet Harritt. The lake was named for Bill Jennings, legal counsel for the HID and vice-president of the California Water Commission.

The Walk
Distance: 3 miles round trip. *Time:* 1.5 hours.

The lake's entire 5.5-mile circuit is open to runners and walkers; we settle for the unpaved portion, 1.5 miles gate-to-gate, following the wide dirt road toward the campground. Campers can start from the campground and do the walk from the opposite direction. Either way, it's a pleasant stroll past laurel sumac, sagebrush, and large clumps of prickly pear cactus.

In spring, the flat spiny pads are decorated with waxy yellow flowers; the dark red oval fruits follow. Both de-spined pads and fruits were eaten by Indians and are still commonly sold in Mexican markets. In summer, look for cottony patches of cochineal scale, tiny insects whose bodies, crushed and dried, produce a natural red dye. Cultivated in Mexico for centuries, cochineal must be tediously hand-picked, with 70,000 insects needed for every pound of dye. Before the development of modern coal tar dyes, cochineal colored pork sausages, soft drinks, cosmetics, and maraschino cherries. With coal tar dyes now linked to cancer, cochineal has been approved by the FDA and could be making a major comeback.

As you walk along, watch for quail, roadrunners, and maybe the pale horned lizard, popularly called a "horny toad," sunning itself by the side of the trail. In winter, you'll see yellow-rumped warblers flashing through the laurel sumac, whose seeds they love to eat. Sumac's dried flower clusters look rather like miniature trees, and they're sometimes used as such in architects' models and model railroad landscapes.

We saw our best and closest osprey sitting on a shoreline willow about 6 feet away from us, coolly surveying the lake. Also called fish hawks, ospreys may be found around any body of water in the county, salt or fresh. Listen for their sweet chirping call, very unhawklike.

We turn around at the gate, where the paved vehicle road begins. You can take one of the small fishermen's paths down to the lake, if you wish, before heading back.

Lake Jennings

BY THE WAY...

Xeriscape Garden and Flume Exhibit

While you're at Lake Jennings, you may want to make a brief stop at the water treatment facility, located on Lake Jennings Park Road, between the campground and the fishing entrance.

Outside is a small xeriscape garden, from the Greek *xeros*, which means "dry," as in Xerox, the dry copier. Xeriscapes are aesthetic arrangements of plants suited to dry climates, needing little maintenance and less water. This one includes Cuyamaca cypress, palo verde, sagebrush, rosemary, sage, and several types of ceanothus.

Across from the garden is a display of part of the old redwood flume, a 35-mile aqueduct built in 1889 to bring water down from the Cuyamaca Mountains to the thirsty citizens of San Diego.

At the flume's grand opening, everyone pronounced the mountain water a great improvement over the San Diego River water they'd been drinking. It later turned out that, for the first few weeks at least, they were drinking the same old stuff after all; engineers had forgotten to install air valves and had to "borrow" river water until the problem was taken care of.

Indian flume-walkers were paid to wade barefoot along the length of the flume, plucking debris out of the water. They were allowed to keep any drowned animals they felt like eating. For awhile, flat boats were tied together and floated down the flume—a cross between a pleasure cruise and an amusement park ride.

A seven-year drought around the turn of the century dried up Lake Cuyamaca, but somehow the flume stayed in operation until 1936, when it was put out of business by the new, nearer El Capitan Dam and Reservoir.

27 LAKE SAN VICENTE

LOCATION

Lakeside. Take I-8 east to Highway 67 and go north. Turn right on San Vicente Avenue and left on Moreno Avenue. Follow Moreno to the entrance and park in the lot (TG1212:A3).

HOURS

Sunrise to sunset, Thursday through Sunday. Same hours, Friday through Sunday, mid-May through September. $5.00/person entrance fee, summer weekends only.

DESCRIPTION

A man-made mountain lake whose pleasant surroundings are still un-touched by major development, San Vicente has only one drawback: it costs $5.00 per person to get in on summer weekends, when the lake is reserved for water-skiing. The rest of the year, there's no admission charge, and for a daily fee California-licensed fishermen can test their skill at hooking trout, bass, and catfish. Rental boats are available during fishing season. For reservations, call City Lakes, (619) 390-0222.

Near the marina, you'll find a concession, a few picnic tables, and restrooms. On the hillside southeast of the parking lot is another small picnic area.

HISTORY

San Vicente Dam towers 200 feet above the streambed of San Vicente Creek. Built by the city of San Diego in 1941–43, it stores water from Lake Sutherland, the Colorado River, and Northern California, as well as local runoff. The lake was stocked and opened to the public for fishing in 1949.

The Walk

Distance: 2.4 miles round trip. *Time:* 1.5 hours.

Drive up the road that winds through laurel sumac and buckwheat, and then drops down to the parking area and marina, about a mile from the entrance.

The trail starts to the left of the parking lot. Take the upper trail, a wide vehicle road opened to cars a few years ago when windsurfers were allowed on the lake. These days, this road to the abandoned windsurfer launch is closed to traffic; it's a good place for a quiet, view-filled walk.

Where the road divides, at the top of the first hill, follow the red "Wrong Way" sign; you're not a vehicle, so you don't have to obey.

These dry, chaparral-covered hillsides are very susceptible to brush fires, as you can tell from the charred remains of shrubs and trees along the way. Before you get to feeling too bad about it, remember that chaparral fires encourage healthy new growth. As you walk on, the vegetation gets taller and thicker, with sumac, chamise, and scrub oak predominating.

There's a short paved stretch at about 0.9 mile. When the paved section ends, you cross over the rocks of a man-made waterfall, flowing just like the real thing. It's the aqueduct outlet, built in 1947.

You'll see tall tree tobacco growing close by and, in summer, down by the water, splashes of magenta canchalagua. You may also see a great blue heron, or catch a glimpse of a pied-billed grebe building a nest in the cattails. Watch the hillsides for rabbits, snakes, lizards—and the occasional coyote.

The road leads down to a picnic table (and portapotty) just at the water's edge. It's a wonderful place to sit and admire the lake and its myriad blue, red, and black-and-white dragonflies, sometimes called "devil's darning needles" because old folk tales say they can sew up the mouths of children who tell lies. This is one of the few places you can be all by yourself by the water, even on a holiday weekend. We found it easy to dream here, and hard to pick ourselves up and get back on the road.

Rounding the first bend on the return trip, you get a good look at the dam and start hearing the sounds of the world again. At about 1.9 miles, you can take the short, rocky drainage path down to the water and follow the fishermen's trail back. On a warm day, it's cooler down here, and you get a different perspective on the lake.

Fence Lizard (left), Alligator Lizard (right)

28 STELZER PARK

LOCATION
Lakeside. Take I-8 to Highway 67; exit at Mapleview Street. Go east to Ashwood, which becomes Wildcat Canyon Road. The park entrance is 2 miles ahead on the right (TG1212:D7).

HOURS
7:30 A.M. to sunset. Parking fee.

DESCRIPTION
This 314-acre regional park has special attractions for children and the disabled, but is a delightful place for any nature-lover to visit. Family and group picnic areas, youth group campsites, hiking trails, restrooms, and play areas are all designed to accommodate wheelchairs. The wheelchair-accessible exercise course is particularly imaginative, and enjoyed by able-bodied children too. For further information, call County Parks, (858) 694-3049.

HISTORY
Once a Kumeyaay campsite, the land was a family retreat for real estate magnate Louis A. Stelzer in the 1940s. It was left to the county on his death in 1972, along with additional funds for its development as a park with facilities for the handicapped. The park was officially opened to the public in 1983.

The Walk
Distance: 1.5 miles round trip. *Time:* 45 minutes.

To the right of the entrance is the Riparian Hiking Trail, which follows the seasonal Wildcat Canyon Creek about 0.7 mile to a hidden picnic site. Along the trail, masses of wild grape hang gracefully from the live oaks, and even on the hottest days, it's shady and cool.

Spring is especially pretty here, with ferns, mustard, and wild radish in abundance, and wrentits, goldfinches, and spotted towhees singing in the trees. Spring is also the time to look for patches of scarlet pimpernel, whose tiny star-shaped flowers are usually scarlet in England but mostly pale coral-colored here. A famous romantic novel written in 1905 concerned a daring Englishman who outwitted the masterminds of the French Revolution and used the flower as his signature and pseudonym. Perhaps he chose the pimpernel because it was an old symbol of assignation. Known to close dependably in late afternoon and in cloudy weather, it has also been called "the shepherd's clock" and "the poor man's weatherglass."

The trail turns left near a tree-shaded table, where you might want to picnic or just spend a few minutes listening for the gnatcatcher's mewing call. Then take the Wooten Loop uphill about 0.2 mile, stopping at the Observation Deck to look for red-tailed hawks. You're out of the trees now and into the sagebrush and buckwheat, with nice views of the surrounding mountains and the gray ribbon of Wildcat Canyon Road. There's plenty of color here in springtime, with purple lupine and snapdragons, golden yarrow, and lavender mariposa lilies covering the hillsides.

Pass the Summit Junction, unless you're in the mood for more climbing and want to go all the way up to Stelzer Summit, another 0.5 mile. About 0.1 mile after the junction, look to your right for a flat-faced boulder with odd, candle-shaped indentations, signs of the dynamiting that once helped to create this trail.

Heading down the ridge back into live oaks, take the high road to the restrooms and playground, completing the loop.

29 OAK OASIS OPEN SPACE PRESERVE

LOCATION
Lakeside. Take I-8 to Highway 67. Go north to Mapleview, turn right, and then turn left on Ashwood, which soon becomes Wildcat Canyon Road. Continue 4.5 miles to Oak Oasis on your left (TG1212:F3).

HOURS

8 A.M. to sunset.

DESCRIPTION

With 397 acres of chaparral and woodlands, Oak Oasis is a fine place to walk. Part of the projected Pines-to-Spines transcounty trail system that will ultimately go all the way from the Torrey Pines State Reserve to Anza-Borrego Desert, it's isolated enough to allow you to see more wildlife and few other hikers. Trails are well marked, but in wet seasons they can turn marshy. There are portapotties across the road at El Capitan Open Space Preserve. For more information, call County Parks, (858) 694-3049.

HISTORY

In the post-Mission days, this area was ranchland. During the gold rush in Julian, a stage ran from Lakeside to Julian, passing through what is now the reserve. In 1940, Margaret Minshall, a high school phys ed teacher, began buying land here and gave the place its name. For years, she ran a summer riding camp for girls and led horse trips from her ranch to the Cuyamaca Mountains. A firm believer in land preservation, she donated her ranch to the county in the late 1980s.

The Walk

Distance: 2.5 miles round trip. *Time:* 1.5 hours.

Start at the information kiosk and follow the wide dirt path through the scrub oak. Bear right, heading downhill to a large, lovely oak grove; these are coast live oaks, not scrub. In spring, you'll see bright red and yellow Western tanagers foraging for insects in their branches.

San Diego Horned Lizard

Keep an eye out for other creatures. On one summer day, we saw a coast horned lizard hiding in some brown, fallen oak leaves, and a large whiptail lizard skittering across the trail. This is snake country too. Watch for rattlers hoping for a taste of one of the gophers that sometimes pop their heads up from their holes all along the trail.

The old log cabin up ahead is the one Margaret Minshall lived in. For years, there was no plumbing or electricity, and she commuted from here to her job at San Diego's Hoover High School, a definite display of voluntary simplicity.

Just before the cabin, there's a turnoff to the Upper Meadow Trail, which rejoins the main trail farther on. We stay on the main trail, crossing a small wooden bridge over what the Minshall family called its "Tule Poolie." It's dry in summer, but winter rains can change that.

As the trail climbs, you get a view of new development. Keep bearing right along the rustic stone wall, and notice on your left the rusty iron posts, chair, and bedstead that are all that remains of the Parents' Roost, the elder Minshalls' weekend cabin, destroyed by a fire that swept through here in 1961.

The cacti you see here are non-natives, part of a cactus garden planted more than sixty years ago.

Back in the open, bypass your next chance at the Upper Meadow Trail (or try it, and circle back here afterwards) and follow the main trail uphill. Take a quick detour left to the Scenic Outlook, where you can stand—or sit—on the large Lakeview Rocks for a sweeping view of Lake San Vicente and its dam, built in 1943 (see Chapter 27) .

The main trail keeps climbing into buckwheat and sagebrush till you pass the Half Way Point sign. Then you start heading downhill, passing through an open meadow which in spring is bright with yellow buttercups and lavender checker-bloom.

Another open stretch, then a small grove of scrub oaks, and the path climbs gently, turning right at the trail sign (left is private property), before heading downhill again. In summer, you'll see what looks like rust-colored fences. As you move closer, you'll see that it's curly dock, a 3-foot-tall buckwheat relative that found its way here from Europe and Asia.

Stop for a shade break in the beautiful oak grove before heading back to the parking lot.

𝟥𝟢 SILVERWOOD WILDLIFE SANCTUARY

LOCATION
Lakeside. Take I-8 east to Highway 67 in El Cajon, then head north to Lakeside. Turn right on Mapleview and left on Ashwood, which becomes Wildcat Canyon Road. From the last turn, it's about 5 miles to Silverwood Wildlife Sanctuary; look for the yellow mailbox and stone gateway on the right side of the road (TG1212:F2).

HOURS
Sundays only, 9:00 A.M. to 4:00 P.M. Closed in August.

DESCRIPTION
These 725 acres of chaparral are owned by the San Diego Audubon Society, which keeps them as close to their natural state as possible. There are several miles of hiking trails, at least 230 species of flowering plants, and 157 bird species. You can picnic near the shady bird observation area by the director's house or close to the parking lot. Volunteers lead guided nature

walks every Sunday at 10:00 A.M. and 1:30 P.M., except in July and August. Organized groups can schedule special tours by calling (619) 443-2998.

HISTORY

Established in 1965, the sanctuary was a gift to the Audubon Society. During the Depression, Harry Woodward, a savings and loan executive, acquired the original 85 acres by paying the back taxes. He built the small house now occupied by the director as a weekend retreat, and from 1934 on kept careful notes on the plants and animals living in the area, including, in the 1940s, his sightings of California condors, probably the last ones seen in San Diego County. Woodward called the place Silverwood because of the silvery look of the sunlight on the leaves of the live oak trees.

The Walk
Distance: 1.5 miles round trip. *Time:* 1 hour.

This trail combo is a good introduction to the varied joys of Silverwood. To start, a short 0.3-mile stroll leads to the director's house and the bird observation area, located by a seasonal creek.

Here you can sit on an odd assortment of donated furniture and watch the winged residents bathe and eat under the tall live oaks. If you enjoy birding, come in the morning, when the feeders are filled. Later in the day, especially when it's warm, birds tend to stay hidden.

At the director's house, you can pick up a map of the park and its trails, copies of the Audubon newsletter, and an assortment of other information.

From the bird observation area, walk east past the water tank and follow the sign to the Cienaga Trail. You'll be leaving the shade and heading through chamise and mountain mahogany, easiest to recognize in late summer and fall, when it's covered with white, curly "feathers," the plumed tails of its seeds.

In spring, you'll be surrounded by scarlet delphinium, blue larkspur, and magenta canchalagua as you proceed into the *cienaga*, or marshy meadow, which can become marshy indeed after rain.

Silverwood is home to thirty mammal species, including foxes and coyotes, whose droppings you can see along the trail. In fall, the droppings are studded with reddish-brown manzanita berries—irresistible, but, apparently, not completely digestible.

After you cross the meadow, the Cienaga Trail turns into the Chaparral Trail. Ahead on your right, almost hidden on the ground, is marker #27, where you'll find holly-leaf cherry. A member of the rose family, it has small whitish flowers in spring, and dark cherry-like fall fruit—a favorite food of many birds and animals. Kumeyaay ate them too, though they're really more pit than cherry.

Stay on the main trail, bearing left; #18 is sugar bush, or mountain sumac, a relative of laurel sumac and lemonade berry, whose tiny reddish berries are also food for birds.

About 0.6 mile in on the Cienaga–Chaparral Trail is a junction; from here, looking north, you can see a Christmas tree farm across the valley. Bearing left on the Chaparral Trail will take you back to the bird observation area; we bear right onto the Sunset Trail, for a bit of local geology.

At viewpoint "A," just on the left, the cleft granite rock dates back to a time 100 million years ago when dinosaurs roamed the earth. Like the other rocks you've been seeing, it's part of the Southern California batholith. The word batholith is a combination of the Greek words for depth—*bathos*—and stone—*lithos*. Our batholith was once a huge mass of molten rock lying deep beneath the ocean floor, extending from Los Angeles County all the way down into Baja California. As the sea level receded and the land rose, the massive rock was exposed to air; eons later, it remains a visible part of our topography.

A piece of the rock; Southern California batholith (Photo by Barbara Moore)

Lichens

At the foot of this venerable boulder, look for delicate bird's foot fern, whose leaf clusters look like tiny bird's feet. You should also find selaginella, a member of the spike moss family that dominated the coal forests millions of years ago, long before the appearance of flowering plants. Popularly called resurrection plant, selaginella looks dead most of the year but turns bright green and springs back to life as soon as it rains.

At "B," look northward to the big squarish rock on whose face is the setting sun for which this trail was named. This sunset is not a carved petroglyph or a fossil, but just one of the interesting patterns produced by ages of weathering.

Walk past the sunset—could it be a sunrise?—and follow the trail right, past more boulders and bird's foot ferns. Mosses and lichens on the trailside rocks can make this section quite pretty in winter and spring. Lichens are some of the oldest plants on earth; here's some doggerel to remember them by: "Annie Algae and Freddie Fungi took a lichen to each other and lived happily ever after in sinbiosis." As a sideline to their mutually beneficial relationship, the algae and fungi in each lichen species produce organic acids, which ultimately break down rocks into soil.

Bear left around a flat granite outcropping to "E," a possible Indian grinding hole, though it does seem far from the creek and rather solitary for the sociable activity of acorn-pounding. It could be a natural depression, made by rainwater and decomposing leaves.

After a view of Wildcat Canyon Road, the Christmas tree farm, and the distant mountains, make your way carefully downhill, staying on the Sunset Trail. Just head toward the sounds of traffic; at the fork pick up the Circuit Trail to the left, which will take you back to your car.

31 HEISE PARK

LOCATION
Julian. Take I-8 east to Highway 67. Go northeast through Ramona, connecting up with Highway 78. At Santa Ysabel, Highway 78 joins Highway 79; continue on to Pine Hills Road. Turn right and follow the brown "Heise Park" signs to Frisius Drive. Turn left on Frisius and go another 2 miles to the park entrance (TG1156:C5).

HOURS
9:30 A.M. to sunset. Day-use fee.

DESCRIPTION
Heise Park includes almost 1000 acres of pine and oak woodlands on the northern edge of the Laguna Mountains. Here, as in the neighboring Cuyamacas, you'll find hot summers, crisp autumns, snowy winters, and plenty of spring wildflowers. The drive itself is a pleasure, winding as it does along tree-lined country roads. Though most of Heise's land is in its natural state, there are campsites for tents and RVs, family picnic areas,

and lovely hiking trails with views of the mountains and desert. Even on crowded weekends, the trails are nearly deserted; our tourist-to-trash estimate tells us that most people seem to prefer sitting around their campsites. On weekdays, it's very peaceful, and you should be able to get a good site without reservations. Cabins are also available. Call County Parks, (858) 694-3049, for further information.

HISTORY

For hundreds of years, Kumeyaay Indians came here in summer, staying to gather autumn acorns and leaving before the cold set in. After gold was discovered in Julian in the 1860s, the area provided lumber for the resulting building boom.

The park's original 200 acres were donated to the county in 1970 by William Heise, a German immigrant who married well, made it big in the hearse business, and patented a number of offbeat inventions including, we are told, the pop-top trash can.

THE WALKS

Pick up a park map at the ranger station; it will give you some idea of how to find your way around. Remember you're in the mountains, well above 4000 feet, and the higher you are, the harder the walk. Just take it easy, and be prepared; carry water in summer, perhaps a small thermos of coffee or hot chocolate in winter. In winter, too, check on snow conditions before starting out. Year-round, wear shoes with good treads, since the paths are steep in places. A walking stick will help you pull yourself up the steep parts, as will the thought that uphill hiking is great aerobic exercise.

Walk 1—Cedar Trail
Distance: 1.3 miles round trip. *Time:* 45 minutes to 1 hour.

Park near the caravan area, not far from the entrance. A short paved service road leads southward through oaks, pines, and incense cedars, whose reddish wood is used in pencils. Just after you pass a pumphouse for the park's water, the dirt trail begins.

For an easier climb, and a very nice side trip, bear left at the signpost. Cross a wooden bridge over the usually dry creek, which could be a flowing stream in winter. One summer day, we ran into a plague of the legendary seven-year locusts here—cicadas, whose mature nymphs were emerging after years underground, sucking root juices and waiting for their chance at adult life. The males were humming all around us, trying to attract females—they sounded like high-tension wires.

Frog pond, Cedar Trail

Meanwhile, every biting fly in the mountains was feasting on our legs, which made taking advantage of the log chairs facing the creek bed impossible. If you're here in early summer, you might consider bringing some insect repellent or wearing long pants. Unfortunately, we didn't.

Head up the stairs through bracken ferns, poison oak, and June-blooming wild roses, which smell even sweeter than they look. There's a second wooden bridge and, to the left, a pond. In summer, it's algae-covered, full of frogs and 3-inch tadpoles, and looks like the primordial soup. You can picture the whole process of evolution here, from the tiny guppy-like tadpoles; to the bigger ones with their first set of legs; to the frogs, newly amphibious, chirping; and finally to ourselves, the ultimate in land animals. At the edge of the water, we considered our roots, locking eyes with the tadpoles, wondering what they made of us.

We saw black-and-white dragonflies here, hovering over the pond weed, and an assortment of butterflies; it was our favorite spot on the Cedar Trail, though not really part of it.

When you're through at the frog pond, cross the bridge and walk uphill to the right. At the next signpost, bear left through the tall trees and poison oak. The path continues uphill and curves south at the park's property line.

Nearby, in spring and summer, you'll find patches of tiny wild strawberries and a number of white fairy lanterns. These lovely white flowers, also called globe lilies, do look like little Japanese lanterns and are one of our woodland favorites.

Keep going uphill and down, enjoying the pine-scented air. At just over a mile, there's a green expanse of bracken ferns. Soon you're at the pump house again, ready to take the path back to the caravan area.

Walk 2—Canyon Oak Trail
Distance: 3 miles round trip. *Time:* 1.5 to 2 hours.

For a longer, more challenging trail, park near youth camp area 2 in the spaces marked "Parking for Hiking Trails," close to the restrooms. Walk uphill and turn right to reach the trailhead, across from site #86. Then follow the arrow 0.5 mile to the Canyon Oak Trail.

In spring and early summer, as you start uphill, look for 3-foot-tall bushes of woolly blue curls, a member of the mint family. The flowers—actually more purple than blue—have long, curling stamens.

The trail leads through oaks and pines, manzanita and mountain mahogany, and then alternates between woodlands and chaparral. Bear left at the first fork—it's less steep this way—and continue to a T-crossing at about 0.3 mile. Then go right; you'll soon be rewarded for your climb with your first mountain views.

Promptly at 0.5 mile, as the sign at the trailhead said, you'll see a signpost pointing left to the Canyon Oak Trail. Heading right leads on to the steeper Desert View Trail, which you might want to try someday.

The Canyon Oak Trail is steep enough for us, and pretty enough too. Bear right at the next signpost and continue on around the loop, unless you're tired. If so, head down about 0.1 mile to Youth Camp 1 and walk back to where we started; this would give you about a mile round trip.

There are rocks and fallen trees to rest on from time to time—just be sure you don't get your hindquarters into any poison oak. At the next signpost, at about 1.4 mile, a short uphill jog to the right will give you a little extra view. Continuing on a few hundred yards, you reach another signpost. Here, you can choose to go left to the Desert View Trail, a fairly steep, shadeless, but view-full 2-mile circuit.

This is usually as far as we go. We take the bypass trail right and then go right again at the next junction with Desert View Trail. This is another good place to look for fairy lanterns in spring and early summer. Heading back, bear right at the signpost to catch that mountain vista again, and then continue left downhill. When you reach the fork, stay on the upper trail—remember, the other is steeper—till you're back at the parking area.

On weekdays, when it's quiet, you should have your choice of large, shady picnic tables. There's nothing like dining peacefully under the oak trees after the trail is done.

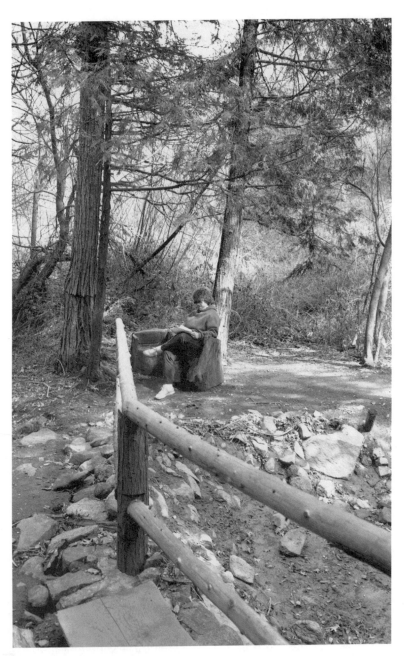

Time out on the trail

ϡℤ CUYAMACA RANCHO STATE PARK

LOCATION

Descanso/Cuyamaca. Take I-8 east to Highway 79 (Japatul Road). Turn left, go under the freeway, and, just after Descanso, turn left again onto Highway 79.

For Walk 1: Turn left on Viejas Boulevard and drive about 1 mile to the parking lot, just after Mizpah Road and before the Descanso Elementary School (TG1216:B2).

For Walk 2: Follow Highway 79 north, passing Green Valley Falls Campground, to the park headquarters, 2 miles ahead on the right (TG1176:G6).

HOURS

Sunrise to sunset. The office at park headquarters is open on weekdays, 8:00 A.M. to 5:00 P.M. Parking fee.

DESCRIPTION

This 26,000-acre park, just 40 miles from downtown San Diego, lies in the Cuyamaca Mountains, whose 6512-foot Cuyamaca Peak is the second highest point in the county (Hot Springs Mountain near Warner Springs is 21 feet higher). Here you can find dense pine and oak forests, broad alpine meadows, and 120 miles of hiking and riding trails. Mountain lions, bobcats, foxes, deer, raccoons, and at least 100 species of birds make their homes here. Both Paso Picacho and Green Valley Falls Campgrounds are excellent for camping or picnicking, with the latter having the advantage of a waterfall. For camping reservations, call (800) 444-7275.

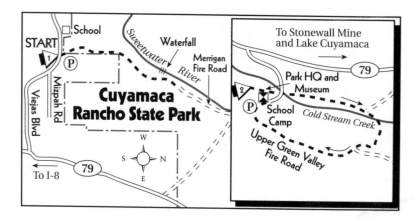

At park headquarters, there is a small museum of Indian history. Stop at the office for information brochures, books, and a detailed map of the park and campgrounds or ask to leaf through the photo album of local wildflowers, organized by color—a great aid to flower identification. You may also want to visit the old Stonewall Mine, a mile south of Lake Cuyamaca, where you can see an exhibit on the history of Southern California's richest gold mine. For additional information on any of the park's facilities, call (760) 765-0755.

Another pleasant stop is Lake Cuyamaca itself. Though not part of the state park, it offers rental boats, good fishing, a 3-mile trail around the lake, and picnicking. Group walks can be arranged by calling the bait shop, (619) 447-8123 or (760) 765-0515.

HISTORY

For at least 7000 years, Kumeyaay Indians lived in this area they called *Ah-ha-kwe-ah-mac*, "the place where it rains." Spanish expeditions found them friendly, but determined to keep their independence. Far from the hub of mission activity, they managed to preserve their traditional lifestyle, continuing to spend summers in the mountains and winters in the desert or near the coast.

Inside the Indian Museum

In 1845, Governor Pio Pico gave Rancho Cuyamaca to Don Augustin Olvera, his niece's husband. Olvera was a prominent figure in Los Angeles politics, and the man for whom the main street of L.A.'s "Mexican quarter" was named.

In the 1860s, when gold was discovered near Julian, hundreds of prospectors and mine workers started pouring in, and the last of the local Kumeyaay were forced out and onto reservations.

In 1885, a dam was constructed at Lake Cuyamaca, a small sometime-lake the Spanish had called "the lake that dries up." Mountain water was brought down to the thirsty city of San Diego by a 35-mile redwood flume. By 1892, the gold rush was over, the Stonewall Mine having produced more than $2 million in gold. The twenty-year-old boom town of Cuyamaca survived for a few years as a summer resort and then disappeared.

In 1923, retired Beverly Hills businessman Ralph Dyar bought the rancho property to use for family vacations. Dyar built the stone house that is now park headquarters and enjoyed entertaining an assortment of movie stars and politicians at his mountain retreat. In 1933, he sold the property to the state for half its appraised value, with the proviso that it be kept open to the public forever.

Walk 1—Merrigan Fire Road
Distance: 2 miles round trip. *Time:* 1 hour.

Walk past the ranger residences, around the gate, and onto a wide, sandy equestrian trail. Soon you'll be on the Merrigan Fire Road, following the upper part of the Sweetwater River, which flows from the mountains into San Diego Bay at Chula Vista. First, though, you have to cross an open meadow, passing live oaks, farmhouses, and probably, red-tailed hawks. After the meadow, continue on through chaparral and oak woodlands. In spring, there's lots of blue ceanothus blooming, along with the usual buckwheat and chamise; in summer, there's gold in these hills—golden yarrow, that is.

The path climbs much of the way, but gradually. You can't really see the Sweetwater River, but you can hear it, along with the squawks of ravens and, in summer, what Tennyson described, onomatopoetically, as the "murmuring of innumerable bees."

At about 0.75 mile, take the first left-forking path downhill for a nice surprise. Turn right again at the bottom, passing through wild roses, poison oak, and, in summer, yellow and white lotus, a member of the pea family. Just ahead is a delightful boulder-encircled pool and waterfall. The signs say "No Swimming," but you can soak your weary feet and stop for a picnic.

In spring, there are green mosses and lichens covering the rocks and ferns growing in the crevices of the boulders. In summer, there's lots of yellow monkey flower. Any time of year, you can watch the water striders skimming the surface and relax for awhile, enjoying the water music, even if you don't feel like picnicking. This is a fine place for reflective moments, and, except on summer weekends, you'll probably have it all to yourself.

A more adventurous way to reach this little oasis is to turn left at the bottom of the path, twice crossing the narrow river on stepping stones that seem to have been set out for that purpose. After the second crossing, just follow the sound of the waterfall. In winter, after rain, this path could be somewhat less practical.

Up at the main trail again, we turn around and head back, but you can continue on along the river if you like. There are some pretty views, and good displays of spring and summer wildflowers, including showy purple penstemon, scarlet penstemon, and heliotrope phacelia, which looks like bushes of purple-headed caterpillars.

For a pleasant addition, about 0.4 mile after the path to the waterfall, there's another turnoff, this one leading down to an old dam. Or stay on the road till, at 2 miles, it forks again, and goes down to the water. Many horseback riders cross here, and head toward the California Riding and Hiking Trail. The Merrigan Fire Road continues right to Highway 79.

Walk 2—Cold Stream Trail

Distance: 2 miles round trip. *Time:* 1 to 1.5 hours.

This delightful trail starts just opposite the front door of the Cuyamaca Indian Museum. Walk down the steps and head north, along a leafy path shaded by tall Jeffrey pines and Kellogg oaks, the only one of our native oaks whose leaves change color and drop off in autumn. Its acorns, sweet and fat, were a Kumeyaay favorite.

Jeffrey pines, whose pitch the Kumeyaay used as glue and whose seeds—pine nuts—were another favorite food, smell distinctly of vanilla. A group of botany students, whose professor had bragged he could always tell a Jeffrey pine by its scent, once sprinkled vanilla flavoring over a number of non-Jeffrey pines on the trail as a joke. The poor teacher was thoroughly confused. Try sniffing a tree trunk for yourself—it's a popular activity around here.

Small signs along the trail describe Indian life and plant usage. As you walk on, listen for the chatter of acorn woodpeckers and the *dee-dee-dee* of mountain chickadees. You may see Steller's jays carrying acorns off to some secret hiding place—so secret that they often forget where it is. These noisy blue jays are thought to be responsible for spreading oak trees throughout the west—the result of forgotten acorns taking root.

You'll soon cross the paved entrance road and pick up the path on the other side. The flat trail following Cold Stream Creek takes you in and out of trees and open areas to the old Indian village site, where you can see two obvious grinding holes in the rock next to the sign.

At about 0.5 mile, you reach a broad meadow, with a good view of Stonewall Peak, named for Confederate general Stonewall Jackson. There's bird's nest thistle here, ground-hugging prickly plants whose green buds and, later, white flower clusters, look like eggs in a nest. Deer like to graze in the meadow; we've also seen bobcats and foxes slinking through the tall grasses.

Cuyamaca is one of the few places in San Diego County where there are still fields of native bunch grasses. Cattle brought here by the Spanish carried European grass seeds stuck in their hair, but even when these took root, they preferred the softer native grasses, and ate them up wherever they found them. The tougher imported grasses, like foxtail and the indigestible ripgut, took over.

In spring, look for the fuzzy gray-green plant called mule's ears—the leaves really do feel like a mule's soft ears. In late winter, they look rather lettuce-like; in spring, they grow taller, with showy yellow flowers. Here too are blue-eyed grass, purple vetch, pale blue wild iris, and magenta owl's clover, a parasite that attaches to the roots of other plants. As summer heat starts browning the meadows, you'll see bright patches of low-growing goldfields, which seem to have been splashed with gold paint.

At 0.7 mile, turn right and head back out of the meadow and up into the trees. We always feel better after hiking here, listening to the wind in the pines and breathing the clear, unpolluted air. The path climbs gradually for a bit, and then descends. Take your time; there are plenty of rocks and stumps you can stop to picnic on, or just enjoy the scenery.

At about 1.2 miles, you'll come to the Upper Green Valley Fire Road. Turn right, and you're on your way back to park headquarters, passing the school camp, where urban sixth graders come to spend their annual week in the mountains. One day, as we were walking by the camp, we saw a mountain lion. Not the usual kind—this one was on a leash, being led around by a park ranger dressed up in a mountain quail suit, for the benefit of a TV crew. The big cat didn't seem to mind the camera, but the presence of the giant quail so unnerved him that he had to be put back in his trainer's van and soothed with a piece of pot roast. Actually, there are many mountain lions in Cuyamaca Park—drawn by the herds of deer that live here. Pay attention.

Mountain meadow

Just before 2 miles, turn right at the fenced swimming pool and head up through the school camp and back to your car.

33 OTAY SWEETWATER REFUGE

LOCATION
Rancho San Diego. From I-805, take Highway 94 going east, turning right at the large shopping center. Turn right again at Singer Lane and then left into the small parking area next to the old Sweetwater Bridge (TG1271:J7).

HOURS
Sunrise to sunset.

DESCRIPTION
With 5600 acres of grasslands, chaparral-covered hills, and shady stream-sides, this part of the San Diego National Wildlife Refuge complex is a welcome addition to our open spaces. Trails will eventually connect with hike-and-bike trails from National City to Cuyamaca. Currently, there are no facilities. For information, call (619) 669-7295.

HISTORY
This southern section of the Sweetwater River, which starts at Green Valley Falls in Cuyamaca State Park and empties into San Diego Bay in Chula Vista, was once an Indian settlement, then a cattle ranch, then slated for housing development. Purchased in 1996 by the U.S. Fish and Wildlife Service as part of the Multiple Species Conservation Program, it has been designated a globally important bird area by the American Bird Conservancy.

The Walk

Distance: 3.5 miles round trip. *Time:* 1.5 hours.

From the parking area, cross the steel Sweetwater Bridge, built in 1929; today, willows, cottonwoods and wild grape poke through its girders. The short stretch of paved road here is a remnant of Old Highway 94. Pick up the unpaved path to your right, and turn right at the fourth utility pole, taking the narrow path into the willows.

Up ahead is a nice, shady glen, which could get pretty muddy in winter. After that, there's a wide trail through open grasslands. The barren, terraced hill to your right is a landfill, where a sprinkler system is trying to make things grow from our trash. Despite the nearness of road and air traffic—you can hear jets on their approach to Lindbergh Field—there's a peaceful feeling here, and the sounds of birds and cicadas prevail.

At the crossing, stay on the main trail, keeping the tree-lined river to your right. Neotropical birds like to nest here. Look for blue grosbeaks, yellow-breasted chats, and ash-throated flycatchers in the cottonwoods and sycamores. Endangered least Bell's vireos are harder to see, but easy enough to hear. Listen for the *deedle-dee-deep, deedle-de-doop* sound they make. Chats tend to call all day long, even when other birds quiet down. If you hear a three-note whistle or a sort of quacking noise, it's a chat.

The soft, ferny, pink-flowered trees are tamarisk, an invasive middle-eastern transplant brought in by early settlers to use as a windbreak. It may

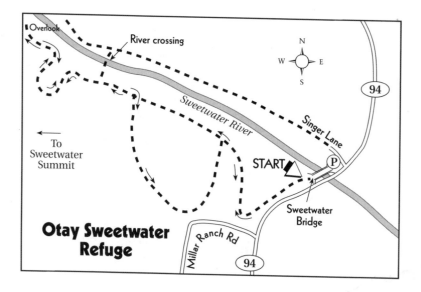

break the wind, but it also adds salt to the soil, and tends to take over wherever it grows. In June, you'll see a lot of wild roses. Year-round, there's plenty of poison oak, so watch your step.

At about a mile, take the right-forking path to the water. You can cross the river here and circle back to the bridge, along the service road. We usually sit on a rock in the shade and listen for vireos before continuing westward along the main trail. As the trail starts climbing, look for redberry, whose bright-colored fruit starts appearing in June.

At the fork, you can go either way. The right fork is shorter and steeper; the left one is prettier, overlooking a small canyon. Look for deer tracks, like large quotation marks on the trail, and the long, slim line that a whiptail lizard leaves.

At about 1.5 miles, you'll come to a vista. You can go on another 4 miles to Sweetwater Summit, or turn around here and retrace your steps to just beyond the optional river crossing. Where the trail forks, go right toward the boulders. At the next fork, go left, heading toward the trees; turn left again, and continue downhill to the junction. Then turn right, and follow your footprints back to the bridge.

Sweetwater Summit County Park

LOCATION
Bonita. From I-805 take Bonita Road east, staying on the south side of the Sweetwater River. Continue straight ahead on San Miguel Road. Turn left on Summit Meadow Road and park in the lot provided outside the campground. No fee, but the park closes at 5:00 P.M. during the week. Call (619) 472-7572 for information (TG1291:B7).

Young herpetologists

DESCRIPTION

This is a different approach to the Sweetwater River, with more wide-open grasslands and chaparral-covered hills. Reservoir views, miles of trails, and a campground make this a popular south-county site. Starting here, you can head for the water tank and a look at the Sweetwater Dam, built in 1888 and washed out twenty-eight years later in the great Hatfield flood (see Lake Morena Park, Chapter 35). Or you can circumnavigate the local golf courses or take the long, often hot, winding road eastward, connecting into the walk we detailed above.

34 POTRERO PARK

LOCATION

Potrero. Take Highway 94 east to Potrero. Go north 1 mile on Potrero Valley Road and east 1 mile on Potrero Park Road to the park entrance. Park near the picnic area (TG429:L10).

HOURS

9:00 A.M. to 5:00 P.M. Overnight camping on weekends. Day-use fee.

DESCRIPTION

A county park way out in the country, Potrero has 115 acres of live oaks, grassy meadows, and good facilities for picnickers and campers. There are ball fields, horseshoe pits, a playground, and a nature trail. For camping reservations, call County Parks, (858) 694-3049.

HISTORY

Before this area was inhabited, Indians used to bring their horses along a rough trail from Tecate, Mexico, to feed in the mountain meadows of Potrero, a Spanish word for "pasture land."

In 1868, one of San Diego's earliest port pilots, Captain C. G. McAlmond, took up residence here. He started a large family, and raised herds of cattle, pigs, and horses.

Mountain lions often preyed on errant livestock, and winter occasionally found valley residents knee-deep in snow. In 1916, Potrero felt the effects of the floods attributed to Charles Hatfield, the rainmaker (see Lake Morena Park, Chapter 35); 2 to 3 feet of water swamped the valley floor, and the roar of the dam collapsing at Otay, 20 miles away, could be clearly heard.

The Walk

Distance: 1 mile round trip. *Time:* 30 minutes.

On the day we first visited Potrero Park, the Society for Creative Anachronism was having a weekend campout. There were 700 people dressed in their versions of medieval costumes strolling through the park, some in full armor. It seems they gather here from time to time, and Potrero's broad fields are certainly a good place for jousting.

In our more contemporary garb, we found the trailhead (with some difficulty) by crossing the group camp area at the northeast end of the campground and following the boundary fence north to the first left, an earthen dam across what was once a water-storage pond.

This really is a "self-guided nature trail": you need to be alert to find it, and there are only a few markers on its whole 1-mile circuit. The first one, on your right, identifies buckwheat, probably the most prevalent plant around.

Standing by the buckwheat, look down at the dead tree beside the dry pond bed; it's a popular perch for woodpeckers and other birds.

Just ahead on the left is another marker introducing you to Eastwood manzanita, which is taller than the coastal variety and has pretty pink flowers and larger berries.

After you cross the dam, take the path to the right. In late spring, you'll see the curly white flowers of salt heliotrope at your feet, and a lot of yellow mustard on either side. Also in spring, look for yellow monkey flower—the wildflower, not the bush. You'll see the foothills variety of bush monkey flower farther on; it's a pale apricot color.

There are several live oaks along the trail, though the next marker is at a scrub oak, about 0.3 mile from the trailhead. Not far away are some bird's foot ferns and the shiny, notched leaves of holly-leaf cherry.

The path you are following is actually a little streambed; in winter, you should see lots of mosses, lichens, and ferns here. In spring and early summer, there's golden yarrow, and the matted orange "witch's hair" of chaparral dodder.

Up a small hill just ahead, beside one of the large granite boulders that are prominent features of this part of the country, is a log bench. You might want to sit down for awhile and listen to the silence. (We, of course, heard distant shouting and sounds of swords and shields as medieval armies clashed on the field behind us.)

When you're ready to get back to the world, walk on through the chamise and the buckwheat. In late spring, keep an eye out for yellow mariposa lilies, whose wide "mouths" have silky hairs to trap pollen from insects' legs.

About 0.2 mile past the bench is another junction; bear right uphill and then downhill. On the right, just beyond the tall flat boulder, you may see springtime clumps of scarlet bugler. Bees love their tubular red blossoms.

Cross the smooth patch of granite and continue on to the wide dirt vehicle road ahead. From here, you can circle back to the group camp where you started out, or head off to the picnic area for an oak-shaded barbecue.

35 LAKE MORENA PARK

LOCATION
Morena Village. Take I-8 east to Buckman Springs Road, go south 4 miles to Oak Drive, then west 3 miles to Lake Morena Drive and the park entrance (TG1296:D5).

HOURS
Sunrise to sunset. Day-use fee.

DESCRIPTION
A 3250-acre recreational area surrounding a 1500-acre reservoir, Lake Morena Park is a popular spot for fishing, boating, windsurfing (summer only), or camping. The lake is stocked with big-time bass, catfish, and

bluegill; fishermen need a state license and a daily permit. Rowboats and motorboats are available for rental on weekends. You can launch your own boat or sailboard for a small fee. There are two camping areas, on opposite sides of the lake, with facilities for group camping and cabins too. Call County Parks, (858) 694-3049, for reservations.

Besides the lake, there is a small museum at the ranger station, full of birds' nests, animal skulls and skins, old farm implements, and an odd collection of barbed wire. There are plenty of picnic tables and barbecues and, best of all, a wonderful, virtually unused trail that half-circles the lake and veers off through pine trees, meadows, and oak woodlands. All in all, a delightful place for day-hiking and feeling you're a million miles away from the crowds—even when the campgrounds are full.

HISTORY

Centuries ago, Kumeyaay Indians camped in the valley that is now Lake Morena. The dam was built in 1902, but the reservoir was never really filled to capacity until January 1916. That's when the city council offered Los Angeles rainmaker Charles Hatfield $10,000 to fill the reservoir.

Hatfield, a sometime sewing machine salesman with a knack for attracting precipitation, set up his "evaporator towers" beside the dam and ended up filling not only the reservoir, but a good part of the county as well. In the downpour that followed, dams burst, bridges washed away,

Charles Hatfield at work in 1916 (Courtesy of the Mountain Empire Historical Society)

Mission Valley was flooded, and a number of hapless citizens were killed. The city refused to pay Hatfield unless he assumed liability, which he was understandably reluctant to do. He went on to other customers, was finally put out of business by the building of Hoover Dam, and took his rainmaking secrets to the grave. A Hollywood version of Hatfield's character can be seen in the movie *The Rainmaker*, starring Burt Lancaster.

The Walk
Distance: 4 miles round trip. Add 1 mile for Ward's Flat meadow loop. *Time:* 2.5 to 3 hours.

Drive in about 0.8 mile from the entrance and park just across from the closed service road, where our walk begins. There's a wonderful display of wildflowers along the trail in spring and early summer; we counted more than fifty different kinds on one June day. We particularly enjoyed the blue ceanothus and the pink-fringed spine flower, a taller, pricklier cousin of Turkish rugging and one of the less common members of the buckwheat family.

The lake is a lovely sight, ringed by mountains, dotted with small boats and, in summer, bright-colored windsurfer sails. Though it can get hot out here, the trail is pleasantly shaded by cottonwood trees; notice their heart-shaped leaves twinkling in the breeze—if there is a breeze. Notice, too, the live oaks, whose leaves are cupped to retain moisture. Keep an eye out for poison oak, which loves to twine itself around their trunks.

After you round the first good-sized cove, you'll see some Great Basin sagebrush, a pale gray-green variety of the more familiar California sagebrush, found along the coast. Our favorite flower on this trail, showy penstemon, blooms in late spring. It certainly is showy, with purple flower clusters on 3-foot stems. The blue delphinium you may see as the road starts climbing is pretty too, but somewhat less spectacular.

The road forks just up ahead. To the left there's only a storage bin; bear right, passing an impressive ruin that was once a retreat for city officials. Built in the early 1920s, it was used for weekend R and R until it burned down twenty years later. The trees nearby are black locust, or false acacia; their fragrant white blossoms appear in June.

Again, the road forks; again, bear right. In spring, look for white-flowered common yarrow, which has a distinguished history. Achilles was said to have used its leaves to stop the flow of blood from the wounds of soldiers—a kind of "Achilles' heal" that gives it its Latin name, *Achillea millefolium.* Early natives of California seem to have applied it to their own cuts and wounds, with equal success, but less notoriety.

If you're on the trail in early summer, don't forget to smell the roses— the wild roses—at about 1.8 miles. If you miss out on the roses, you can still admire the trees, like the oval-leafed Engelmann oaks, named for the nineteenth-century German botanist who was actually an expert on cacti.

Pretty soon, you'll start seeing the lake again. Notice the "ghost trees" in the water, with pale dead algae hanging from their branches. These trees were actually drowned when the water level was higher, and their roots and branches can be a real hazard to boaters, windsurfers, and fishermen.

You should see some wildlife as you're walking: a red-shouldered hawk flying over the lake, a mottled gopher snake slithering across the grounds, flashy red and blue dragonflies along the water's edge. Pass a metal storage shed and some power poles and continue uphill for a fine view of the dam and the mountains. Hold onto your hat! It can get windy here.

Follow the road downhill, as it curves past massive granite rocks and over to the dam. Look westward into the boulder-strewn valley—the result of dynamiting to build the dam. The dam itself would be a great place to sit and watch the sun go down, if you're camping at the lake. On a moonlit night, you might not even need a flashlight for the trip back.

The return trip is uphill, but not enough to make you pant, and generally shady. Our last time here, we had the unexpected bonus of seeing one of our favorite reptiles—the ring-necked snake, a small, slim, charcoal-colored snake with a red belly and a red neck band. When defending itself, this little snake coils its tail up into a knot and then, uncoiling rapidly, gives the startling effect of a big red, hungry mouth.

When you reach the main road again, you can take a left and head back the way you came, or go right through meadows and woodlands to Ward's Flat. This 1-mile loop is well worth the extra time; we love it.

You can picnic under the Coulter pines, where bright yellow orioles and black phainopeplas like to nest. It's so peaceful out here, you probably won't feel like rushing back. Just don't let any of the giant pinecones fall on your head; they're called "widow-makers" because their scales end in sharp, curved talons that could do some serious damage to your skull if you happen to be in the right place at the wrong time.

When you're ready, cross over the flat area to the east side of the meadow and head back along the vehicle road.

From this side, you get a good look at the rocky hillsides to the west, especially Morena Butte, a massive rock towering over the meadow. Look for raccoon, coyote, deer, horse, and bike tracks along the trail—they'll give you an idea of who's sharing the road with you.

At the triangular "057" sign, you reach the end of the loop and rejoin the main road again. Continue gently up and downhill for the rest of the trail.

If you're ready for another hike—not necessarily at this very moment—Lake Morena Park connects into the Pacific Crest Trail, which goes from the Mexican border all the way to Canada. The section here is more difficult and not as varied as the trail we've just taken, but if you're up for it, give yourself plenty of time and water—and enjoy! Look for the PCT sign near the park's entrance.

Part III

WALKING SHORTS
A Bundle of Extras for More Walking Pleasure

By the Shores of San Diego: A Beachcomber's Guide

San Diego's greatest treasure is its beaches—76 miles of them, from the Orange County line to the Mexican border—and we all have our favorites. Families like La Jolla Shores and Coronado's Silver Strand; surfers like Trestles, north of Camp Pendleton, Swami's in Encinitas, the south end of Del Mar, and Windansea in La Jolla; singles head for Pacific Beach and Mission Beach.

In low tides, if you're feeling ambitious, and you don't mind getting your feet a little wet, you can actually walk all the way from Oceanside to the south end of La Jolla Shores, and from Coronado to the border. Check your tide tables, and plan to be back before the tide comes in.

Summer beaches are generally wider, sandier, flatter, and more crowded. In winter, storms can strip away as much as 15 feet of sand, exposing a surface of cobblestones (making walking more adventurous) that won't be covered over again until summer. The damming of our rivers has kept sand from replenishing itself naturally and has led to major problems with beach erosion.

But winter is really the best time for beachcombing. The storms that ravage our beaches wash up wonderful stuff to rummage through: perfect sand dollars, for example, those relatives of sea urchins and sea stars, which, when alive, are covered with downy, purplish-gray spines that help them burrow down into the sand where they live.

And shells: knobby Kellett's whelks and wavy tops, nice 3-inch and 4-inch specimens, and light brown bubble shells, as well as the ubiquitous and often colorful scallop shells. Now and then, you can find a wavy top operculum, the protective trapdoor the living animal uses to seal up its shell, which looks like a wavy bit of shell itself.

Winter is also the time for tidepooling and whalewatching (see "Exploring Tidepools" and "A Word About Whales"), but any time of year is fine for birding. At the water's edge, you can usually see sandpipers and sanderlings scurrying about on quick little feet and lazier sea gulls hoping for a handout. Overhead, there are often flocks of pelicans flying in a rough V-formation, searching the waves for schools of anchovies, their favorite food.

Sometimes there are pods of playful dolphins surfing just offshore. Don't mistake them for sharks just because you see their dorsal fins; these large gray animals are intelligent mammals, and not at all dangerous. A more

A whale's tail (Photo by George Zucconi, courtesy of the San Diego Natural History Museum)

common hazard than sharks is stingrays, which lie invisibly on the ocean floor and can perforate your foot if you step on them. It's always a good idea to shuffle your feet when you walk into the water so they know you're coming and can get out of the way.

Another of our favorite local marine mammals is the California sea lion, seen occasionally swimming near the surf line or resting on a rock. Just south of the Children's Pool in La Jolla, you can usually find quite a few of them, along with harbor seals, basking in the sun on what is called—though they share it with seabirds—Seal Rock.

If you want to tell the seals from the sea lions, harbor seals have rounder heads and no ear flaps; their short front flippers look like paws. Sea lions have more dog-like faces and long front flippers; by folding their back flippers under their bodies, they can "walk" on land. Sea World's performing seals are actually California sea lions.

You may see round translucent blobs of jellyfish washed up on the sand; even when dead, they can still sting, so don't pick one up to examine it. Kelp is another beach phenomenon; odd lengths of these large brown algae frequently break off from our offshore kelp forests. You'll most likely notice three kinds: 150-foot-long strands of giant kelp, with large ridged "leaves" and small, pear-shaped floats that pop when you step on them;

feather boa kelp, which looks just like its name; and bull kelp, with a single melon-sized float and a long, leafless strand that makes a perfect beach jump-rope.

The algin found in kelp is used in a staggering variety of products, including chocolate syrup, toothpaste, beer foam, ketchup, finger paints, floor wax, hand lotions, and cosmetics. Kelco, a local company, regularly harvests the prolific giant kelp, which can grow as much as 2 feet a day. Kelp is 92 percent water, so harvesting must be done on a large scale, but cutting the top few feet off the kelp canopy encourages replacement growth.

If you happen to be in the right place at the right time, you may get to witness the spectacular late-night spawning of hundreds of tiny grunion (see "A Word About Grunion," below). But even if you miss the grunion, there's always the human carnival of surfers, beach bunnies, fishermen, kayakers, joggers, and just plain folks who frequent our beaches every day.

Here are a few of our favorite spots, and their main attractions.

Kids and kelp (Photo by Barbara Moore)

36 HARBOR BEACH

LOCATION
Oceanside. Parking near Harbor Drive South (TG1085:H6).

DESCRIPTION
Heavily de-sanded by storms and the building of the harbor, much of this wide beach's white sand was brought in by truck. Walk south, skirting the mouth of the San Luis Rey River to the Oceanside Pier, or beyond. The paved promenade along the Strand from 9th Street to Wisconsin is especially good for wheelchairs.

37 FLETCHER COVE PARK

LOCATION
Solana Beach. Parking at the end of Plaza Street (TG1167:E7).

DESCRIPTION
In the 1920s, Solana Beach developer Ed Fletcher used hydraulic water pressure to cut an opening from the bluffs to the sea, so residents of his community could have an ocean view. Walk north to the tidepools at Cardiff's Table Tops reef, or south to the San Dieguito River in Del Mar, where a path leads up to tiny, bluff-top Woodward Park, where the remains of 10,000-year-old Del Mar Man were found in 1929. From here, there's a 360-degree view of the coastline, racetrack, and, in winter, migrating gray whales. The north strip of beach can be nonexistent in high tides; check your tide tables before setting out.

38 NORTH TORREY PINES BEACH

LOCATION
Del Mar. Parking along North Torrey Pines Road or in the large parking area (fee in summer) off Carmel Valley Road (TG1207:G1).

DESCRIPTION
A popular family beach, good for swimming and boogie boarding. Walk north to the river mouth in Del Mar, passing tidepools and the remains of an old public pool built to keep swimmers and stingrays—" the dread stingarees"—apart. Look for sun-bleached sand dollars along the way. Walk south for impressive sandstone bluffs with 50-million-year-old fossil

oysters, clams, and snails embedded in them. In low tides, continue on to Black's Beach and La Jolla Shores. You can vary the return by detouring through Torrey Pines Reserve, taking the steps just north of Flat Rock.

39 KELLOGG PARK

LOCATION
La Jolla Shores. Parking in the lot off Camino del Oro (TG1227:H5).

DESCRIPTION
Good swimming and boogie boarding; crowded in summer. There's a grassy picnic area and a short paved promenade, good for wheelchairs. To the north are Scripps Pier and the tidepools at Dike Rock. To the south are more tidepools, just below the Marine Room. This beach is a favorite of scuba divers, who explore the kelp forests of its offshore underwater reserve.

A Word About Grunion

Do you believe in grunion? They do exist, even if you've never seen them, and every year, in spring and summer, they come up on our sandy beaches for an amazing, all-out spawning spree.

Around midnight, just after high tide on the nights following a new or full moon, thousands of these 6-inch silvery fish start making their way ashore—somewhere.

Stranded on the sand, the female digs in below the surface to deposit her eggs, while the male wraps himself around her to fertilize them. It's a live fish sex show, and you'd be very lucky to see it.

When their spawning is over, the grunion are ready to catch the next wave back to sea, unless prevented by frantic humans splashing through the shallow surf, armed with flashlights and buckets, trying to scoop up the wet wriggling bodies with their bare hands. This is the only legal way to catch grunion, and you still need a California fishing license. If you do happen to get your hands on a bucketful, grunion are delicious dipped whole in flour or cornmeal and fried—except in April and May, when they're protected by law, and can only be observed.

Whatever month you choose, it's anybody's guess whether the grunion will show up on a particular beach or a particular night, so warm clothes, a hot thermos, and a philosophical attitude are definitely in order.

Local tide tables will give you the dates and times of predicted runs, but there are no guarantees. Only the grunion know when and where they are actually coming ashore.

40 TOURMALINE SURFING PARK

LOCATION
Pacific Beach. Parking at the end of Tourmaline, off La Jolla Boulevard (TG1247:G5).

DESCRIPTION
Look for fossil scallops in the bluffs just south of the parking lot. Walk north past tidepools to False Point, south to Crystal Pier or all the way to the Mission Beach jetty. There's plenty of action on the Pacific Beach boardwalk.

41 SILVER STRAND STATE BEACH

LOCATION
Coronado. Parking (fee in summer) in the lots off the Silver Strand, Highway 75 (TG1329:D1).

DESCRIPTION
Wide, sandy family beach, usually uncrowded. Walk north to the Hotel Del Coronado or south to the Imperial Beach Pier. Good winter shelling. Look for endangered Western snowy plovers.

─ A Word About Whales ─

Every winter, thousands of California gray whales pass by our beaches on their annual southward migration. When the storm season begins in the icy Bering Sea, these massive mammals head for the warm lagoons of Baja California, where they mate, calve, and rest for awhile before starting the long trip back in the spring.

Pregnant females leave first, then courting trios—a female and two randy males. Females are kept very busy during breeding season, entertaining male after male on migration and in the calving lagoons, where occasionally newborns are squashed by the amorous activity. It was previously thought that one of the males helped the other get into position, and kept him in place. But as naturalists have recently pointed out, there are no known animals that need help with their coupling.

Last to join the migration are the one- and two-year-olds, still sexually immature. Some never make it all the way to Baja, preferring instead to dawdle along the California coast.

On the southern leg of the journey, the whales swim close to shore, following coastal landmarks, and sometimes poking their heads up for a quick look around, a behavior called "spyhopping." More often you'll see a spout—the whale's exhalation of air and water. If you're very lucky, you'll see a whale "breaching"—hurling its bus-sized body out of the water. Some scientists think this could be a kind of "jumping for joy."

It's a long trip, and gray whales are not built for speed. Moving along at 4 or 5 miles an hour, it takes them about three months to cover the 5000 miles to Baja.

Because they swim so slowly, white star-shaped whale barnacles are able to attach themselves to the whale's blue-black skin, giving it a grayish appearance. Orange whale lice also come along for the ride, settling in near the blowholes. Seen up close, the whale's body is a mottled mass of parasites.

Winter whale-watching cruises give you a chance to get a good look at the California grays. Birch Aquarium and the Museum of Natural History offer naturalist-led weekend trips in January and February. If you can't make one of those, there are a number of sportfishing outfits in Mission Bay, San Diego Bay, and Oceanside that offer daily cruises. Just look in the Yellow Pages under "Fishing Parties" and choose the most convenient. Reservations are a must, and so is warm clothing; it can get cold and damp out there while you're waiting to see a spout.

For landlubbers, there are good vantage points at the Carlsbad Seawall, Swami's Park in Encinitas, Seagrove and Powerhouse Parks in Del Mar, Torrey Pines State Reserve, Coast Boulevard in La Jolla, Cabrillo National Monument in Point Loma, and Border Field State Park in Imperial Beach. Piers and beaches are also good places for whale watching, though in recent years, whales have been staying farther offshore, probably to avoid all those whale-watching boats. During migration season, Cabrillo offers daily whale talks and films—call (619) 557-5450 for details.

More about whales:

- All whales are descended from the same primitive hoofed animals as cows, goats, and sheep.
- About half a gray's weight is fat, or blubber. A 6-inch layer keeps them warm in the Arctic and gives them energy for their long journey. During the eight months away from their home waters, they eat little or nothing, saving themselves for summer gorging.

- Gray whales may weigh as much as 40 tons and grow as long as 50 feet, but they can't swallow anything big; their esophagus is only the size of a baseball. They live off some of the smallest creatures in the ocean—tiny shrimp-like amphipods, or krill—but they can put away a ton or two of these a day.

- Gray whales have no teeth; instead they have baleen, a set of fringed plates that look like hemp curtains and work to filter out mud and seawater and trap food inside their mouths. Whalebone, once found in combs, umbrella spokes, and ladies' corsets, is actually baleen. The expression "I'm going to whale the daylights out of you" came from the use of whalebone for buggy whips.

- A gray's gestation time is about 13 months. The newborn calf is 14 to 15 feet long and weighs 1500 to 2000 pounds—about the size of a compact car. It can consume 50 gallons of its mother's milk every day, and gain 2 or 3 pounds an hour! Whale milk is about 40 percent fat, really more like whipped cream.

Exploring Tidepools

If you don't mind getting your feet wet, walking slowly, and bending down a lot, tidepools are something you should definitely look into. Generally speaking, there are two high and two low tides every day, with the highest and lowest occurring at the time of the new or full moon. Low, or minus, tides expose the rocky reefs along our shores, giving us a look at many marine animals we never get to see outside of an aquarium.

Tidepooling is free, fascinating, and addictive, especially in winter, when minus tides tend to come at convenient afternoon hours. It's best to go out when the tide is still receding, about an hour before low tide, so you'll have plenty of time to explore; pick up a tide table at your local lifeguard station, bait-and-tackle shop, or surf shop, and plan ahead. New Year's Day usually has a good low tide, and tidepooling is one of our favorite ways to start off the year.

Start at the Spray Zone, reached only by the highest tides. Here are tiny black periwinkle snails, volcano-shaped buckshot barnacles, and insect-like isopods, which will actually drown if immersed in water.

In the lower High Tide Zone, covered and uncovered by water every day, you'll see blue-black mussels, attached to rocks and each other by byssus fibers, used in the Mediterranean in ancient times to make cloth of gold. There are hundreds of green anemones here, animals that look more like flowers.

Touch one gently near its mouth center and it will close around your finger, expecting lunch. Smaller prey than we are paralyzed by the poison darts in the greenish tentacles, and sucked into the anemone's stomach. All we feel is a faint stickiness, not at all unpleasant.

On your way to the Mid-Tide Zone, hermit crabs will probably catch your eye as they scurry about in their borrowed seashells, looking for food. The snails that were the shells' original occupants moved a lot slower, and ended up in the bellies of voracious sea stars—starfish—which spit out the shells when they finished eating.

Clinging to the rocks are limpets and armor-plated chitons; under ledges, look for honeycombed colonies of sandcastle worms.

The Low Tide Zone, exposed on minus tide days, is where most of the really exciting stuff is. Here, in the shallow pools, are spidery brittle stars, spiny sea urchins, wavy top snails, the large brown shell-less snails called sea hares, which can grow up to 35 pounds, and even a few shy octopuses. There are red and orange bat stars too, though pollution and warmer water seem to have depleted their numbers.

Beach walkers

Most of these animals are not in plain view, but have to be uncovered. A whole world can be found by turning over a rock, but don't forget to replace the rock when you're through looking, or the animals won't survive your visit.

Resist the temptation to take anything home with you; our local marine life is protected. We like to carry clear plastic cups to keep interesting specimens in seawater while we observe them face to face. If you do the same, be sure to put everything back where you found it, and *don't* leave your cup on the beach.

Serious tidepoolers come prepared for a wet walk. Wear old tennis shoes that still have some tread to them, and shorts or long pants you can roll up. Try leaving a dry pair of shoes and socks in the car to change into; after an hour or two of tidepooling, there's nothing like the joy of warm feet. On winter days, a thermos of something hot is welcome too.

If you're ready to tidepool, here are some of San Diego's best sites.

42 SWAMI'S PARK

LOCATION

Encinitas, just south of the Self-Realization Fellowship on Highway 101. Limited parking in the lot, or park on the street (TG1167:B1).

DESCRIPTION

A small grassy park above a popular surfing beach, Swami's is named for Swami Yogananda, founder of S.R.F. (see Self-Realization Fellowship Meditation Gardens, below, under "Secret Gardens"). There are restrooms, picnic tables, and steps going down to the beach. North of the steps, there's nearly a mile of reef, where you can find sea hares, brittle stars, bat stars, octopuses, and an occasional seal.

43 SOUTH CARDIFF STATE BEACH

LOCATION

Solana Beach, south of Restaurant Row in Cardiff. Easy access and a lot of parking. Parking fee (TG1167:D6).

DESCRIPTION

A good place to take children. South of the parking lot, there's 0.25 mile of reef with lots of hermit crabs, sea hares, crabs, anemones.

Sea-sculpted sandstone (Photo by Barbara Moore)

44 SOUTH COAST BOULEVARD

LOCATION
La Jolla, south of Cuvier Street (TG1227:E7).

DESCRIPTION
Smooth sandstone rocks and small sandy coves. Dark algae-covered patches are slippery when exposed. Heading south, there's 0.5 mile of reef, with deep, narrow channels, where garibaldi, opal eye, and sea hares graze.

45 FALSE POINT

LOCATION
Between Bird Rock and Pacific Beach. Access on Sea Ridge Drive and Linda Way, off La Jolla Boulevard (TG1247:G5).

DESCRIPTION
Steps down to the rocky shore, some rock scrambling. About 1.5 miles of reef. Sea urchins, hermit crabs, abalones, and nudibranchs.

Tidepools at Cabrillo

46 CABRILLO NATIONAL MONUMENT

LOCATION
Point Loma. No parking fee in lower tidepool area (TG1308:A3).

DESCRIPTION
About 1 mile of reef to explore. Best finds are around the point, about 0.5 mile in. Large chitons, whelks, colorful nudibranchs, and giant sea hares. Ranger-led tidepool walks (see Cabrillo National Monument, Chapter 8).

Bayside Ambles, Seaside Strolls

47 OCEANSIDE HARBOR

LOCATION
Oceanside, Harbor Drive (TG1085:H5).

DESCRIPTION
A 2-mile paved path circles around from the Villa Marina Hotel to South Harbor Drive, passing sailboats, shops, restaurants, and an assortment of gulls and pelicans along the way. There's ample free parking east of the railroad tunnel and there are restrooms, ramadas, picnic tables, and a playground.

Walk on the beach or the jetties, or stroll around the marina—a nice, flat place to ride bikes too. In winter, whale-watching cruises leave from Helgren's Sportfishing (760) 722-2133.

48 CARLSBAD SEAWALL

LOCATION
Carlsbad Boulevard near Ocean Street (TG1106:E7).

DESCRIPTION
The Great Wall of Carlsbad is a corridor of sand-colored concrete between the bluffs and the beach, and a good place for a paved beach walk, as long as you're tall enough to see over the 4-foot wall.

This is actually an erosion control project, designed to keep the bluffs from crumbling down. It's a good place to see some of the sand-dune plants that beachfront development has been bulldozing away.

From spring through fall, look for the magenta flowers of sand verbena, trailing its oval-leafed vines down the bluffs. There's sea rocket too, a white-flowered relative of wild radish, and yellow beach lotus, a member of the pea family.

Probably easiest to recognize is statice, popular with bees and florists; its long-stemmed purple flowers rise from a clump of large, curly leaves.

There are patches of bright green New Zealand spinach, with its small, spade-shaped leaves, and usually a lot of tumbleweed, that typical Western

plant that's really an immigrant—Russian thistle—with appropriately red stems and red-tinged white flowers. As it ages, tumbleweed turns into a dry, spiny mass that blows in the wind, scattering thousands of seeds as it tumbles along.

The seawall is a fine place for watching shorebirds, dolphins, whales, surfers, and sunsets, and can be pretty exciting in high tides, with the waves splashing against it.

The city of Carlsbad put in a pedestrian path along the overlooking stretch of Carlsbad Boulevard, so you can take the high road one way and the low road to return, for a distance of about 1.25 miles.

49 LA JOLLA COAST WALK

LOCATION

Torrey Pines Road at Coast Walk, a small street between La Jolla Shores and Prospect (TG1227:F6).

DESCRIPTION

This beautiful half-hour cliffside walk is a little hard to find the first time, but once you've found it, you won't be sorry. There are spectacular views of the ocean, La Jolla Shores, and the bluffs of Torrey Pines and the north coast; on a clear day, you can see all the way to the Encina Power Plant in Carlsbad.

Parking is the biggest problem. There are a few spaces near the "Ecological Preserve" signs and about 0.1 mile farther in, but these are often taken. Parking in town near the caves is even more difficult; you may want to try starting from whatever spot you can find on Coast Boulevard.

Alternatively, you can park at La Jolla Shores and walk down the beach as far as the Marine Room, where you can cut up to Spindrift Drive, which becomes Princess Street. Turn right onto busy Torrey Pines, and continue south about 0.3 mile to the walk's beginning.

Whatever way you get there, you'll be strolling between the villas and the deep blue sea, with benches along the way so you can sit and admire the view. Just keep following the trail along the cliff's edge to the grove of Torrey pines above the Sunny Jim Cave, where bootleggers reportedly stashed their liquor during Prohibition.

Leave nothing but footprints . . .

50 LA PLAYA

LOCATION
Point Loma. Park on Talbot Street and Anchorage Lane, near the San Diego Yacht Club (TG1288:B3).

DESCRIPTION
La Playa—"The Beach" in Spanish—is Point Loma's best-kept secret, a lovely 0.5-mile stretch of shoreline between two yacht clubs, passing some of the best-kept lawns and stateliest homes in San Diego. There's a real Mediterranean feel to the view southward—a green hill (*loma* means hill) covered with red-roofed houses, looking down on the picture-pretty cove with its rows of silvery masts.

A century and a half ago, hides were tanned and beef fat melted down into tallow on these shores, waiting for tall ships to carry them away. Then, the area was known as Hide Park. Today, the occasional sunbather dozes on a beach towel by the water, her ship having already come in, and you see the kind of lush subtropical plantings that used to be found only in Hawaii.

This path is popular with lunchtime walkers. It comes out to the street just past tiny La Playa Yacht Club, but you can continue on along San Antonio, about four-and-a-half short blocks.

On the corner of San Antonio and Owen there's a huge, fantastic pink-barked eucalyptus spreading across the street—a favorite daytime perch for night herons. At Kellogg Street, you're back on the *playa* again, with another 0.25 mile of quiet beach ahead. Here, you can inspect the bayside rocks for scurrying shore crabs and look across the channel to Shelter Island.

51 SHELTER ISLAND BAYSIDE WALK

LOCATION
San Diego. Take Rosecrans to Shelter Island Drive. Park at the circle where the road ends, near the Friendship Bell tower and the Harbor Police (TG1288:B4).

DESCRIPTION
Shelter Island was born in the 1950s after wartime dredging deepened the bay for Navy ships and heaped up enough mud to create a pleasure island of hotels, restaurants, and yacht clubs, connected to the mainland by a causeway.

Near the flagpole, just south of the Harbor Police building, you can sit and watch boats going by, and admire the homes of Point Loma's La Playa section across the channel. Also across the channel are the docks of the Nimitz Marine Facility of Scripps Institution of Oceanography. If any of Scripps' research vessels are in town, this is where you'll find them.

If you have good eyes, you can see the caged sea lions, used by the Navy for deep-water research; you can hear their barking when the wind is right. To the south is the entrance to San Diego Bay, where you'll often see big ships coming in. It can get pretty windy out here, but otherwise it's a

Tunamen's Memorial

wonderful place to pass an hour or two, with convenient picnic tables, benches, restrooms, and even telephones along the promenade.

Start your walk with a look at the Friendship Bell, presented to San Diego by the citizens of Yokohama, Japan.

At about 0.3 mile is the bronze Tunamen's Memorial, surrounded by thorny natal plums, with sweet-smelling, jasmine-like flowers and round red fruits. Notice how it takes three men to hook one tuna, as it did before the huge nets called tuna seines revolutionized tuna fishing. San Diego was once America's tuna capital until the decreasing tuna population, foreign imports, and stringent U.S. laws protecting dolphins accidentally caught in the seines led to the canneries' closing and the industry's decline.

A 0.5-mile stroll will bring you to the Shelter Island Fishing Pier, where you can usually get a good, close look at some of our local pelicans that like to perch on the pier or the low roof of the snack bar, hoping for a handout. In the 1970s, these big-billed birds with 6-foot wingspans were considered an endangered species. Toxic residues of DDT in the fish they ate had led to a thinning of their eggshells; eggs were often too fragile to survive the parent's weight during incubation. More recently, pelicans seem to have made a remarkable recovery, managing to adapt and survive like the rest of us.

Another 0.5 mile brings you to the boat launch area near the Bali Hai Hotel, a logical turnaround point.

52 HARBOR ISLAND DRIVE AND SPANISH LANDING PARK

LOCATION
San Diego, south of Lindbergh Field (TG1288:E2).

DESCRIPTION
Close to the airport, Harbor Island isn't quite as peaceful as its landfill twin, Shelter Island, but it's still a good place for bayside walks.

At Harbor Island Drive, park near Tom Ham's Restaurant at the west end. As you walk along the paved promenade, you'll be looking across at the hangars and installations of North Island, San Diego's naval air base, and moving toward the downtown skyline and the Coronado Bay Bridge.

Here in the bay, you can see aircraft carriers and destroyers, cruise ships and freighters, mixing in with the small pleasure boats of weekend- and weekday-sailors.

There are benches along the way, restrooms, and some green grass to soften the concrete ribbon. A good turnaround point is the parking lot at the Reuben E. Lee; if you get this far, you'll have come about 1.5 miles.

At Spanish Landing Park, where Vizcaino is said to have landed in 1602, start your walk at the lot at the west end of Harbor Drive. From here, you can see the small boats and large hotels of Harbor Island. There are grassy areas, occasional benches, restrooms, and bike racks too; unlike Harbor Island Drive, Spanish Landing is open to cyclists.

It's about 1.5 miles to the turnaround at the east end, or you can head south and continue around, connecting into Harbor Island Drive.

53 BAYSHORE BIKEWAY WALKS

LOCATION
Imperial Beach and Coronado.

DESCRIPTION
Because of its importance to migrating and nesting birds, more than 2000 acres of South San Diego Bay were designated as a National Wildlife Refuge in 1999. The 27-mile Bayshore Bikeway, once a railroad line that brought lumber to the Hotel del Coronado, is now a good place for hikers and bikers to explore the Silver Strand. Even when the beaches on the west side of the Strand are crowded, you can have these bayside walks virtually to yourself. Access to most of these locations is easiest going from south to north on Highway 75, the Silver Strand.

Walk 1—South San Diego Bay Refuge

LOCATION
Imperial Beach, north end of 7th Street off Highway 75 (TG1329:G6).

DESCRIPTION
This is a great birding site. You can walk either way from here along the bikeway, scanning the water for pelicans, egrets, terns, and black skimmers that nest on the dikes to the east, where the salt works, San Diego's oldest industry, can be seen. Look for the telltale white pyramids of salt extracted from the diked ponds. Birds like it here because of the plentiful seafood—brine shrimp and brine flies that inhabit the salty ponds.

Walk 2—South Bay Marine Biology Study Area

LOCATION
Coronado, near Imperial Beach. Access from Highway 75. Look for the small parking area at the edge of the bay (TG1329:F4).

DESCRIPTION

These 27 acres of county-owned wetlands are home to many marsh-loving birds. At low tide, stroll out on the dikes jutting into the bay to see shorebirds, diving ducks, black skimmers, and the small, dark sea geese called brant.

Walk 3—Beach Lotus Trail

LOCATION

Coronado, north of Imperial Beach. Access from Highway 75, at Attu Avenue, just north of Coronado Bay Road (TG1309:D6).

DESCRIPTION

A 1-mile loop trail through flat dunes, starting from Silver Strand naval housing. Two low tiled walls give an artist's view of local bay life. Look for yellow-flowered beach lotus in summer and long-eared black-tailed jackrabbits year-round.

Walk 4—Nature's Bridge to Discovery

LOCATION

Coronado. Access from Highway 75 at Fiddler's Cove. Park in the small bayside lot (TG1309:C5).

DESCRIPTION

From the marina, go north past the fenced-off preserve where snowy plovers and least terns are encouraged to nest. This 1.4-mile wheelchair-accessible path is meant as a natural complement to the man-made Coronado Bridge, ahead in the distance. Native plants like dune primrose have been planted, and the dunes are enhanced with imported sand. Observation decks enable walkers to survey the area and watch nesting birds.

Immature gull

Walk 5—Tidelands Park

LOCATION
Coronado, first right turn after crossing the bridge. Or stay on Highway 75 (Orange Avenue) and turn right on Second Street and follow it to Glorietta Bay Boulevard, turning right and then left into the park entrance (TB1289:A6).

DESCRIPTION
A pleasant park in the shadow of the Bay Bridge, with broad grassy areas, a small sandy beach, playgrounds, and a sweeping view of the bay, the bridge, and downtown San Diego, Tidelands is a good spot for a walk, a picnic, or a bike ride. The path goes under the bridge and through a fenced-in section along a golf course before connecting into the bikeway. Watch for kingfishers, herons, and other water birds; they seem to like it here too.

54 CHULA VISTA MARINA (BAYSIDE PARK AND LAUNCHING RAMP)

LOCATION
Chula Vista, between J and G Streets, off Marina Parkway (TG1329:H1).

DESCRIPTION
Bayside Park is a pretty city park with green grass, bay views, picnic tables, a paved jogging/walking/biking/skating path, restrooms, and a concession. Walking out on the concrete pier, you can see Imperial Beach, Mexico, and sometimes, the Coronado Islands, a Mexican wildlife refuge. Walking back, you see downtown San Diego, framed by the Coronado Bridge.

You can watch fishermen trying their luck in the bay, where it's probably luckier not to catch anything, since it's still one of the most polluted on the West Coast. As on all public ocean piers, no fishing license is required.

A stroll through Bayside Park takes you past an RV resort and marina where you can admire the boats and feed the ducks—you can even buy duck food at the concession.

Half a mile south is the Chula Vista Launching Ramp, whose marshy south side is a good place to birdwatch. Many shorebirds visit the mudflats here at low tide; migrating ducks come here in winter. Park in the first lot and walk around the perimeter, with grass, picnic tables, and benches along the way.

Upstream, Downstream

55 OAK RIPARIAN PARK

LOCATION

Oceanside. Access off Lake Boulevard at Ridge Road (TG1107:E3).

DESCRIPTION

From the grassy area with its playground, picnic tables, and restrooms, you can take a walk on the wilder side. Cross the creek, heading right past the live oaks and into a more open area of toyon and laurel sumac. This trail can be muddy in winter, but in dry times it's pleasant. Keep bearing right, passing through meadows of yerba mansa, whose white flowers with yellow cone centers can be seen in spring and summer, and whose large leaves turn red in early fall.

At about 0.5 mile, you'll come to an open section with powerlines up ahead. Take the low path, keeping the creek to your right, and head for the hills, crossing through the chaparral. Soon you'll see Lake Calavera; take the path to your right that leads toward it, and connect into the lake circuit (see "Great Lakes" below).

Creek crossing

56 BUENA VISTA PARK

LOCATION

Vista. Take South Melrose north to Shadowridge Drive; go left to Antigua Drive and the parking area near the pond (TG1107:H5).

DESCRIPTION

Buena Vista is a pretty neighborhood park with a small pond that offers some very good birding. Besides numerous mallards and coots, you'll see herons and red-winged blackbirds. In spring and summer, look closely at the water. This is one of the best places to see baby coots, as distinct from their black, white-billed, red-eyed parents as they can be. For the first few weeks of their lives, they're small, downy, and colorful, with an orange mane, a red and orange bill, purple eye patches, and a gray and yellow body. Both parents take turns feeding the baby choice bits of algae. As it grows older and larger, it loses its color, and turns gray all over. Not until the bird is a year old does it develop the characteristic coloration of the adult.

The dirt trail here, dedicated on Earth Day in 1991, starts near the portapotties and picnic tables, and leads alongside eucalyptus trees. In spring, white bush lupine blooms here—a good opportunity to see this rather rare plant. Further on, to your right, is the gate to Dawson Los Monos Canyon Reserve, part of the University of California's Natural Reserve System. A wonderful mix of peaceful streamsides, oak woodlands, and chaparral, the reserve offers guided walks from time to time. Call (858) 534-2077 for information.

The trail crosses a wooden bridge over the creek before looping back to the parking lot. You can, if you wish, take any of the offshoot trails before heading back.

57 CARMEL VALLEY CREEK

LOCATION

Del Mar. Park on the west side of Carmel Country Road, about 0.1 mile past the Palacio Del Mar complex, near the "Mt. Carmel Ranch" sign (TG1188:C7).

DESCRIPTION

More than 5 miles of equestrian, hiking, and biking trails through mixed native and non-native greenery make this area a delight for local walkers. As a result of mitigation for construction of Highway 56, the creek bed has been planted with oaks, sycamores, cottonwoods, and willows, while Torrey pines and a sprinkling of broom and sages fringe the parallel paved and unpaved paths.

About 0.2 mile in, the dilapidated wooden tower and outbuildings mark the place where the Carmelite Sisters of Mercy started a convent and dairy farm in 1905. The nuns supplied dairy products and produce to Mercy Hospital in San Diego. Just beyond is the white, Victorian-style ranch house they lived in until the late 1940s. The large cross on the north side of Highway 56 is the Carmel Valley Cemetery, where several Sisters of Mercy are buried, along with some of the families who lived and died here in the 1900s. It's an ecumenical graveyard, with Catholics buried on the west end, Protestants on the east.

You can walk all the way to I-5, though we prefer turning around at the cattail-fringed pond that egrets seem to like. If you don't mind the noise and the buildings, the end of the path is another 0.2 mile ahead.

You can also access this path midway at Carmel Creek Road and Tang Drive; look for the green "Bike Route" sign and start out in either direction.

The trail leads eastward under the Carmel Valley Creek Bridge to another, more developed pond in the heart of the Palacio Del Mar housing complex. Ducks, green and blue herons, and white egrets can usually be found here; it's a lot more suburban and the walk may flood out in the rainy season, but weather permitting, you can keep going for another mile or so. Just stay on the path; everything else is private property.

58 MORRISON POND

LOCATION
Bonita. Access off Sweetwater Road, just west of Briarwood (TG1310:H1).

DESCRIPTION
Once the site of a sand and gravel operation, the area around small, green, willow-fringed Morrison Pond has been cleaned up and opened to walkers as part of a mitigation deal for the building of Highway 54. Now there's a 1-mile path that crosses the often-dry Sweetwater River and circles the water. Though it's in between busy Sweetwater and Bonita Roads, the pond has a country feeling. In summer, when the exploded seed pods of the willows hang from their branches like cotton, there are shady groves just off the path that will make you feel as if you're in back in the bayous. In winter, some of these groves may be underwater; in dry seasons, they're great for secluded picnics.

Great Lakes

59 LAKE CALAVERA

LOCATION
Carlsbad. From Lake Boulevard, take Sky Haven Lane south to Azure Lado Drive. Park along the street (TG1107:C3).

DESCRIPTION
Recent development has surrounded this storage reservoir, but the 3-mile circuit trail is still good for walking and a good place to see wintering redhead and canvasback ducks. Follow the main trail heading west toward the dam. After you cross the dam and head eastward, the lake turns back into a creek. Along the way, you'll see plenty of toyon, also known as California holly. In summer, it's covered with white flowers. Robins, finches, and mockingbirds come here to feast on the red berries that start appearing in the fall.

You can take this trail all the way to Oak Riparian Park (see "Upstream, Downstream") or, just after the powerlines, look for a small path heading into the trees to find the creek crossing that will lead back to where you began.

60 DISCOVERY LAKE

LOCATION
San Marcos. From San Marcos Boulevard, turn south onto Bent, which becomes Craven Road. Then turn right on Foxhall Drive, in the Discovery Hills housing development, and park at the end of the road, near the lake (TG1128:G3).

Hottentot Fig, a.k.a. ice plant

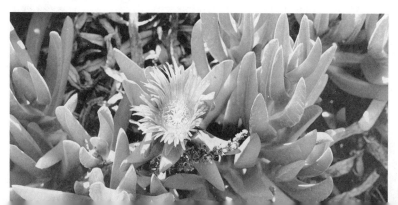

DESCRIPTION

A pleasant suburban lake popular with stroller-pushing moms, local jog-gers, and mountain bikers, Discovery Lake offers a flat, paved 0.8-mile cir-cuit or a more challenging uphill climb leading into the 3-mile Double Peak Trail, with broad views of the area from the top of the ridge. Burnt tree skeletons on the hillsides are evidence of the disastrous Harmony Grove fire that swept through here in October 1995 and helped clear some of the brush from the ridge, making trail building a little bit easier for the California Department of Forestry.

There's an attractive park and playground area at the trailhead, with restrooms and picnic tables. The one drawback is the sound of the sand and gravel company at the lake's north end, grinding up rocks to make concrete for the next new developments. If you like silence, come on a weekend, when even rock breakers take a break.

61 LAKE WOHLFORD

LOCATION

Escondido. Main entrance on Lake Wohlford Road, off Valley Parkway (TG1110:J2). The lake is open daily 6:00 A.M. to sunset, closed from early September to late December. For information, call (760) 839-4346.

DESCRIPTION

A pretty lake, popular with local fishermen, Lake Wohlford has pleasant trails for walkers. By the time you read this, the 1.3-mile Kumeyaay Trail, which follows the lake's north shore, should be completed; at this writing, it still involves more bushwhacking than we can recommend.

Our current favorite is the mile-long Egret Trail, accessible from Oak-vale Road, on the lake's south shore (TG1110:J3). Turn left at the metal gate just before Oakvale Lodge. Ignore the old private property sign; this is public land. Park in the lot and follow the oak-shaded path, stopping to read the informative signs. At about 0.1 mile in, there's a bench overlooking the lake and an Indian grinding hole; Kumeyaay and Luiseño gathered acorns here centuries ago. A nutritionally rich food that made up about half their diet, acorns were second only to salt among foods prized and traded by native Californians.

A bit farther on, make your way up and over a rock outcropping and pick up the path again; a lone portapotty marks the end of the trail. Walk down to the lake and see if you can spot some white egrets, or just enjoy the view before heading back.

62 LAKE MIRAMAR

LOCATION

Scripps Ranch, entrance on Scripps Lake Drive (TG1209:G3). The lake is open Saturday through Tuesday for boating and fishing, except in October. Walkers can come in every day, sunrise to sunset; park in the large parking area.

DESCRIPTION

A city reservoir popular with fishermen and picnickers, Lake Miramar has several picnic areas, a concession, and a boat dock where you can rent a boat or launch your own. For reservations, call (619) 390-0222.

As on all city lakes, fishermen need both state and daily permits, available at the concession. There are restrooms near the entrance, and portapotties strategically located along the paved lake road.

The area here was once part of Rancho Miramar, the 4000-acre retreat of newspaper tycoon E. W. Scripps, whose older half-sister, the reclusive Ellen Browning Scripps, became San Diego's leading philanthropist. Across the street from the entrance, beyond the fenced-in pond, you can see the remains of a stone wall on the property where E. W.'s daughter, Nackey, lived for many years. Her husband, Tom Meanley, had been Scripps's secretary. When the two eloped in 1916, the old man was infuriated, but he still left them a fine piece of real estate, which their heirs sold in 1985 for $11 million.

Park and take the paved path heading west toward the dam. Don't be

Bobcat

put off by the "Keep Moving" sign—it's for fishermen, who aren't supposed to fish beyond the gate.

This is one of the few dams in the county that people are allowed to walk across. High above Mira Mesa, you can look westward to Mount Soledad in La Jolla and, on clear days, the Pacific Ocean. Here, where no cars are allowed, you'll usually find other walkers, joggers, in-line skaters, and cyclists sharing the road with you.

If you're lucky, you'll see a pair of brown-and-white ospreys that roost nearby and come here to fish for their food. In spring and summer, there are families of mallards and coots swimming in and out of the cattails. In winter, you'll see long-necked Western grebes and black-and-white lesser scaup. Rangers tell us that bobcats and coyotes come out of the hills at night to feed on the water birds.

At about 0.5 mile, on the north side of the dam, the road turns east and continues another 0.75 mile until it joins the vehicle road. Here are many of the usual chaparral plants—chamise, monkey flower, manzanita, golden yarrow, black sage, and scrub oak. In late spring, the north slopes are covered with bright magenta canchalagua. On the hilltops across the lake is the newer growth typical of the area—pink and gray housing developments.

This is where we turn around and head back. But you can continue another 4 miles around the lake on the vehicle road, or the pleasant dirt trail below, stopping at one of the picnic areas for lunch.

63 LAKE MURRAY

LOCATION
La Mesa, entrance on Kiowa Drive (TG1250:F7).

DESCRIPTION
Lake Murray, located in the most developed section of Mission Trails Regional Park, is a city reservoir with ducks to feed, birds to watch, and a paved shoreline trail to follow. The trail, more of a road really, is a fairly flat 3.5 miles each way, and is popular with joggers, fitness walkers, and bike riders. It's especially pleasant on wheels; kids might want to try it on skateboards or skates.

On the southeast side of the lake, not far from the entrance, are picnic tables, barbecues, and restrooms. Currently, fishing and boating are permitted on Wednesdays, weekends, and holidays, except in September and October. Bring your own boat or rent one; call (619) 390-0222 for reservations and (619) 668-2050 for other information.

Once part of the nearly 60,000 acres of grazing lands owned by the San Diego Mission, this was the site of La Mesa Dam, built in 1895, and now buried beneath the waters of Lake Murray. The present dam was built in 1918, and extended in 1953. For twelve years, the lake was closed to the public because of an infestation of hydrilla, an annoying weed that clogs irrigation canals, spoils water quality, snags hooks and lures, and winds around boat propellers. It was reopened in the spring of 1987.

The lake circuit is not a particularly "wild" walk—almost everything here was recently planted and is carefully maintained—but it's a pretty spot. In winter, hundreds of gulls have taken to visiting here. In spring, the soft cooing of mourning doves will accompany you as you walk. You might see a roadrunner dart out in front of you. Keep an eye out for rabbits and lizards too.

In spring, the area is bright with yellow Caltrans daisies and mustard. You'll appreciate the occasional shade of a pepper or eucalyptus tree, since it can get pretty warm here on a sunny day, especially when you're walking on asphalt.

There's plenty of chaparral broom, sagebrush, prickly pear, and some castor bean trees, with a few ornamentals like coral and silk oak trees planted in between. On the northeast side, you'll find yourself practically in people's backyards, as you head toward Cowles Mountain, the highest point in the city, once used by Kumeyaay as a solstice observation site.

At the 1.5-mile marker, the road turns west. To your right, behind fencing, is a golf course; watch out for stray balls. If you go all the way, there are two eucalyptus groves and a picnic area near the end of the road that would make good rest stops before heading back.

64 CHOLLAS LAKE

LOCATION
College Grove. The park entrance is at 6350 College Grove Way (TG1270:D7). Open 6:30 A.M. to sunset.

DESCRIPTION
This 60-acre urban wilderness is a mecca for runners and fitness walkers. At 7:00 A.M. and 5:00 P.M. there are dozens of people doing laps around the lake—a 0.75-mile circuit. Parking at these times is next to impossible; you may have to park outside on the street. Seniors especially love Chollas, since it's a good, safe place to practice a daily exercise program. The lake is open for fishing to kids under sixteen. Semiannual fishing derbies are held in March and November, and there have been some record catches.

Originally built in 1900, Chollas was an active reservoir until 1952. The only city lake not operated by the Water Utilities Department, it's a Parks and Recreation project. Besides being a good place for large and small pic-nics, with the usual picnic tables, barbecues, and playgrounds, and a lot of shady eucalyptus trees, Chollas offers a wealth of special activities: canoe-ing classes, model plane and boat clubs, and a summer day camp. For in-formation, call (619) 527-7683.

In addition to the lake circuit, there's a 0.5-mile nature trail, starting just past the covered picnic tables, to the north of the parking lot. Trail guides should be available at the trailhead, or ask at the office.

Cross the wooden bridge over a rock-lined stream—actually an irrigation ditch. There are plantings of non-native ferns, philodendrons, and jade plants growing between the rivulets—definitely more of man than nature here.

As the trail climbs gently, curving westward, things start looking a little more "natural." You'll see prickly pear, buckwheat, laurel sumac, and the *chollas,* or jumping cactus that the lake is named for.

Just past Mouse Mesa are some benches where you can sit unobserved and watch a birdbath where goldfinches, hummingbirds, scrub jays, and mockingbirds often drop by for a dip or a drink. Farther on, there's a cactus garden, and beyond that, a small lushly planted section. There's mint grow-ing in the little stream, and, above the pastel lantana, a tall clump of purple-flowered marsh fleabane.

Up ahead are some benches with tree-branch backrests you might want to try out before heading down to the lake. Another 0.5 mile takes you around it, and gives you a chance to do some duck-watching as you walk. At the north end, there are steps leading up to Gloria's Mesa, a fanci-ful playground/picnic area named for a local community leader, and a path leading down into the 80-acre canyon area which will someday include ballfields, more playgrounds, and developed trails.

Family outing

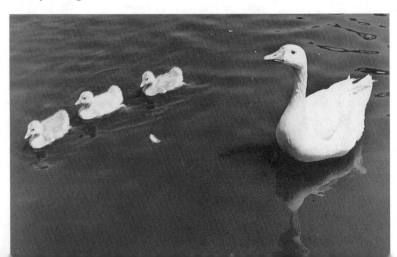

65 SANTEE LAKES

LOCATION
Santee. Entrance on Carlton Oaks Drive (TG1231:A6). Open 8:00 A.M. to sunset. Parking fee.

DESCRIPTION
Part of a 190-acre property owned and operated by the Padre Dam Municipal Water District, this chain of seven small lakes offers fishing, boating, camping, and a lot of onshore activities in a quiet suburban setting. Lakes are stocked with trout and catfish. Rowboats, pedal boats, and canoes are available for rental all summer long and on winter weekends. Volleyball and horseshoe equipment can be rented too. There are playgrounds, group picnic areas with barbecues, and a general store where you can buy fishing permits, state licenses, food, drink, and a variety of picnic and camping supplies. Lakes 6 and 7 are reserved for the exclusive use of campers; the other five lakes are open to all, and can be hiked or biked around.

To us, this park's most attractive feature is that it's all done with reclaimed sewage water—a useful and beautiful solution to our water shortage problems. Another attractive feature: handicapped access throughout the park. For information and reservations, call (619) 448-2482.

Park beside the first lake. Here you have a chance to get up close to some of Santee's coots, which are practically tame. You can look right into their beady eyes and marvel at their three-lobed chartreuse toes.

The paved 2.3-mile vehicle road around Lakes 1 through 5 doesn't need much instruction—just park and go. This is a good place for a bicycle; walkers would do well to stay on the grass, and out of the way of cars.

The main facilities are near Lake 5, at 0.8 mile. This is about the only place in the county you can see multicolored wood ducks that lay eggs in nest boxes put out by the California Waterfowl Association. Look for them in the water or in the trees. At 1 mile, turn left—only campers can continue straight ahead. Stop by Lake 6 to do some birding. Hundreds of water birds like to congregate here, especially in winter on fish-stocking days. More than 175 species of water birds and perching birds have been recorded at Santee Lakes—you should see quite a few.

Several of the lakes have little islands, suitable for picnics. On the west side of Lake 5, you can cross an arched bridge onto an island of live oaks left over from the original streamside setting.

This far side of the lakes is less traveled and more peaceful, but you'll have to cross back between Lakes 1 and 2 to return to your car.

66 LINDO LAKE

LOCATION

Lakeside, entrance on Lindo Lane (TG1232:B3). Open 9:00 A.M. to 5:00 P.M. weekdays, 9:30 A.M. to 7:00 P.M. weekends. Walkers and cyclists can come in before 9:00 A.M. if they park outside.

DESCRIPTION

Lindo means "pretty" in Spanish, and Lindo Lake, maintained by the county and run by the Lakeside Community Service Association, is a pretty place to barbecue, fly a kite, or feed the ducks. There are picnic and play areas, a ballfield, tennis courts and horseshoe pits, and, of course, the lake, which is open for fishing year-round. Pedal boats are available for summer rental. For information, call (858) 694-3049.

Originally dedicated as a public park in 1886, when the new township of Lakeside was promoted as the Pasadena of San Diego County, Lindo Lake is one of the county's few natural freshwater lakes. The luxurious Lakeside Inn, built here in 1887, was meant to rival the Hotel Del Coronado, and featured golf links, tennis courts, outdoor dining, and boating on the lake.

In 1904, the inn's new owner claimed the park and lake as part of his property, fenced it all in, and built a racetrack around the lake. Barney Oldfield, designer of the original Oldsmobile, competed here, along with other famous race car drivers.

In 1916, a group of citizens sued to get their park back. They won, and the irate owner died soon after, stipulating in his will that the inn was to be demolished.

Feeding ducks at Lindo Lake

In the 1940s, construction of the Chet Harritt Dam and Lake Jennings cut off Lindo Lake's main source of water, and one good drought turned the lake into a dry hole. Since then, well water has been pumped in to maintain a reasonable level, and murky water and rapid algae growth have been persistent problems.

Today, there's a new filtration system, part of a master plan to rehabilitate the lake and create new park facilities, including a landscaped 2.5-mile trail. For now, you can circle Lake 1 ("Little Lindo") and Lake 2 ("Big Lindo")—each a 0.75-mile circuit—and walk out on the peninsula, about 0.3 mile.

All walks start from the ranger station; all are paved and handicapped accessible. "Little Lindo" is the least traveled. Cross the small bridge and pick up the trail to your right, taking a left around the lake, past willows and cattails, and back out to the main road again. From here you can continue on around "Big Lindo," passing closer to the street and various forms of "civilization"—a sometimes rowdy parking lot, group picnic areas, a community center, restrooms, a ballfield, and lots of ducks, geese, coots, and cormorants. Back at the ranger station, take a left onto the peninsula for a visit to the old boathouse in the middle of the lake, where you can watch the ducks, the park's perimeter, and the distant mountains.

67 OTAY LAKE

LOCATION

Chula Vista. Take I-805 south to Telegraph Canyon Road, then head east 9 miles. Telegraph Canyon becomes Otay Lakes Road and intersects with Wueste Road. Take Wueste south to the reservoir entrance; the park is 2 miles farther on (TG1332:B3).

DESCRIPTION

Lower Otay Lake is a city reservoir that's walker-friendly, with more than 3 miles of dirt trails winding partway around the large, pretty lake. It's open Wednesday, Saturday, and Sunday for fishing and boating, but walkers can park outside and use the trails anytime. For more information, call (619) 390-0222.

This is a great spot for birding. Besides the always-hungry "funny ducks" and geese at the boat dock, former Easter pets discarded by their owners, look for ruddy ducks, pintails, and shovelers in the water, as well as herons, egrets, and grebes. Hawks and owls, and even a pair of golden eagles, seem to like the trees here. If you see dark, turd-like objects under a eucalyptus, they're regurgitated owl pellets, with undigested skeletons of tiny rodents inside. At least one of us thinks these are a real find.

Eucalyptus grove

The 70-acre county park is open daily from 9:30 A.M. to 5 P.M., with a $2.00 parking fee. It has a nice developed section, and a mile-long loop through the caravan area, where you can see Donovan Prison in the distance and hear rifle fire from the sheriffs' shooting range; there's also a short, worthwhile walk to a close-up view of the dam. Start across the road from the playground and head uphill to a low stone wall where you can sit and admire the lake, the pinkish humps of the Jamul Mountains, and of course, the dam.

The area around here has seen its share of climactic events. Nearby Otay Mesa was the site of the first controlled heavier-than-air flight in 1883. John Montgomery, for whom Montgomery Field in Kearny Mesa was named, flew his glider a full 600 feet, cruising 15 feet above the ground, twenty years before the Wright brothers' flight.

In 1916, rainmaker Charles Hatfield succeeded spectacularly in his attempt to end a drought. The original dam at Lower Otay burst, flooding the valley with 13 million gallons of water, washing houses out to sea and killing a number of people (see Lake Morena Park, Chapter 35). Construction of a new dam began later that year and was completed in 1919. Remains of the old dam can still be seen at the west side of the new one.

The park is part of the 8000-acre Otay Valley Regional Park, which will someday extend from San Diego Bay to the reservoir. For now, if you want more activity, visit the nearby Olympic Training Center which offers hourly tours beginning at 9:00 A.M. They'll even let you walk around their 0.8-mile track. For information, call (619) 656-1500.

Ocean Piers

Fishing piers aren't just for fishing—they're good for walking too. You can watch dolphins, surfers, and whales from our ocean piers, and get a gull's-eye view of the shore. If you're fond of fishing, public piers are the only place you don't need a license.

68 OCEANSIDE MUNICIPAL PIER

LOCATION
Oceanside, at the end of 3rd Street. Closed during storms (TG1105:J1).

DESCRIPTION
Oceanside's first pier was a commercial wharf built in 1885, near what is now Wisconsin Street; two years later, it was a mass of rubble. Since then, several other piers were built and destroyed by storms, including the 1132-foot recreational pier built here in 1927.

Reopened in 1987, the pier is now 1942 feet long, with restrooms, a bait-shop, and a restaurant at the end. Names of all local donors are engraved into the wooden railing; it's nice to see so much community support.

If you don't feel like walking, a "people mover" will taxi you from one end of the pier to the other for 25 cents—but only during restaurant hours.

69 CRYSTAL PIER

LOCATION
Pacific Beach, at the foot of Garnet Street (TG1247:H6). Open 7:00 A.M. to sunset.

DESCRIPTION
Only 720 feet long, the Crystal Pier was 1000 feet until the winter of 1982–83 when stormy seas claimed a chunk of it. The motel here is the only place in California you can sleep over the ocean. Just past the motel are bait, snack, and souvenir concessions.

The Crystal Pier opened in 1927, its main attraction a deluxe ballroom with crystal chandeliers and a cork floor to keep dancing feet from getting tired. Unfortunately, the ballroom wasn't braced properly, and all but the hardiest dancers became seasick as they whirled around the floor.

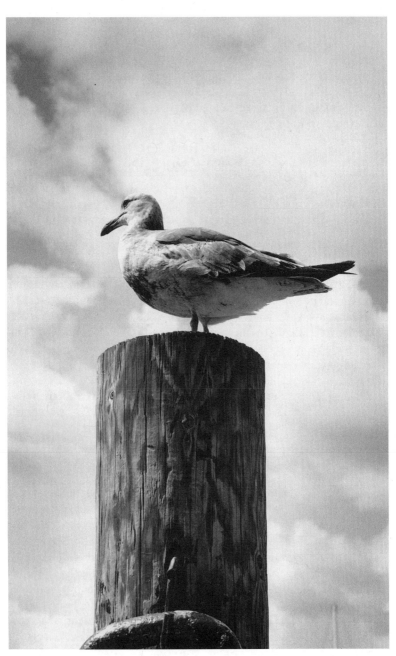

Seaside sentinel

In a few months, the pilings were riddled with holes from boring marine worms; no one had thought to coat the pilings with protective creosote.

The entire pier was condemned and not reopened again until 1936; the cottages were a new addition. Over the decades, storms subjected the pier to damage. The cottages have been upgraded, and the pier is still a pleasant if creaky place for a short walk and a backwards view of the busy beach scene.

70 OCEAN BEACH MUNICIPAL PIER

LOCATION
Ocean Beach, at the foot of Niagara. Stair access from the parking lot at Newport (TG1267:H6). Closed during storms.

DESCRIPTION
Built in 1966, this T-shaped concrete pier extends 1971 feet into the ocean. We've seen lobster, stingrays, and halibut caught here. There's a bait shop, and a restaurant, usually with a pelican or two on the roof. From the end, you'll have a good view of surfers riding their waves into the beach.

71 IMPERIAL BEACH MUNICIPAL PIER

LOCATION
Imperial Beach, at Seacoast and Evergreen (TG1349:E1). Closed during storms.

DESCRIPTION
Built in 1909 to lure would-be home buyers from Imperial County to the beach, Imperial Beach's original pier was designed to generate electricity with the Edwards Wave Motor, which used the energy of the waves to turn generators. It was a good idea, but it didn't quite work out.

The old pier, however, survived until the winter of 1982–83, when severe storm damage shut it down. The new pier, more than 1000 feet long, includes a bait shop and restaurant. At the approach to the pier is a colorful public sculpture called "Surfhenge," four giant translucent acrylic surf-board-shaped arches installed in 1999 as a tribute to Imperial Beach's proud surfing heritage. Half a century ago, Imperial Beach was the birthplace of big-wave surfing in California.

Secret Gardens

72 ROSICRUCIAN FELLOWSHIP GARDENS

LOCATION
Oceanside. 2222 Mission Boulevard, at Amick Street (TG1086:C5).

DESCRIPTION
The International Headquarters of the Rosicrucians was established on this mesa top in 1911, four years after founder Max Heindel inspired the creation of the Fellowship of the Rose Cross.

Park in the guest parking area, and look for the "Meditation Walk" sign at the north side of the lot. The paved, 10-minute walk leads to the rose gardens near the twelve-sided temple, whose shape represents the twelve signs of the zodiac. From there, you have a broad view of the San Luis Rey Valley below.

There's good birding along the way. You should see Western bluebirds and other migratory birds, especially if you come in the morning or late afternoon.

73 QUAIL BOTANICAL GARDENS

LOCATION
Encinitas, on Quail Gardens Drive, north of Encinitas Boulevard (TG1147:D6). Open 9:00 A.M. to 5:00 P.M. Admission fee. For information, call (760) 436-3036.

DESCRIPTION
These lovely gardens feature 30 acres of palms, ferns, hibiscus, bamboo, and hundreds of other exotic plants from all over the world. There are natives too, but the exotics here are much more interesting. Come on a weekday morning, when there's no one else around, and you're likely to see a family of quail skittering across the path; after all, this is Quail Gardens.

Even if you don't see quail, you should hear them. Listen for the call "*Cuidado! Cuidado!*" which means "Be careful" in Spanish. Once this sentry call is sounded, the rest of the covey clicks softly to each other, making sure everyone gets the message.

Check the "What's Happening" board outside the gift shop for lectures,

Agave

concerts, plant sales, and other events. Free docent-led tours start here every Saturday at 10:00 A.M., weather permitting.

Don't miss the Mildred MacPherson Waterfall, framed by tropical foliage—a peaceful place to dream away a few moments. Follow the falls down to a water lily pond, where you'll often see the resident turtle sunning himself or swimming through the murky water. There are koi here too, those colorful Japanese carp that can live as long as a human and cost as much as a house.

In spring, the pond-side jacaranda trees are covered with purple blossoms. When the blossoms fall, you can see flowering bromeliads, called "air plants," growing in the jacaranda branches.

Make your way downhill to Palm Canyon, where, in summer, you'll see orange dates in the tall palms and on the ground; they look more like apricots than the brown oval fruits we're used to.

In the South African section, along the service road, there's a pink-flowered virgilia that local birds really love. On our last trip, we saw Allen's hummingbirds courting here, the male doing a series of dramatic swoops to impress the female. There were at least a dozen or more bush tits and goldfinches in the branches, searching for edible insects.

Nearby are the proteas, those unbeautiful, oddly endearing flowers that look like artichokes, corncobs, oversized bottle-brushes—anything but flowers.

On one visit, we had a thrilling bit of good luck. Just behind the gift shop, as we were leaving, we saw a gray fox, probably on its way to sample some of the fallen dates in Palm Canyon. Here's wishing you the same happy serendipity!

74 SELF-REALIZATION FELLOWSHIP MEDITATION GARDENS

LOCATION
Encinitas, 215 K Street. Look for the gilded lotus domes of the S.R.F on Highway 101 (TG1167:B1). Open 9:00 A.M. to 5:00 P.M., Tuesday through Saturday, 11:00 A.M. to 5:00 P.M. Sunday.

DESCRIPTION
A quiet spot, beautifully landscaped, with an unbeatable view of the sea, this is a fine place for watching surfers, dolphins, whales, and early sunsets. Off-limits to the public, except on Sundays, is the hermitage built for Swami Yogananda (1893–1952), founder of the S.R.F, who loved to meditate here. Local legend has it that this spot was once a power place for California Indians, long before the swamis discovered America.

Flowering plants are changed regularly, so the garden looks a bit different every time you visit. Don't miss the koi ponds, full of large, lovely fish. Strategically placed stone benches are often occupied by meditators, but you can usually stake one out for yourself. The beach below is called, not unnaturally, Swami's, and has some of our favorite tidepools (see Swami's Park, in the earlier "Exploring Tidepools").

Wild Wings: A Birder's Guide

Like walking, birding is one of the most popular outdoor activities in the U.S. today. San Diego is a paradise for birders, with nearly 500 species of birds to be found throughout the county. Any one of our walks can be turned into a bird walk with the proper equipment—a pair of binoculars and a field guide. Here are a few good places for beginners to try.

75 BUENA VISTA LANDING AND HOSP GROVE

LOCATION
Carlsbad. Access at Jefferson/Marron Road (TG1106:E3).

DESCRIPTION
Part of Buena Vista Lagoon, the creek's widest part and California's first ecological reserve, the landing is a popular duck-feeding spot. Besides the "funny ducks"—offspring of wild mallards and pet ducks—and some sizable geese, there are wilder birds you can see. Look for pink-legged stilts in the shallows, and pied-billed grebes farther out on the water.

A reported 200 species of wildlife can be found here—we assume that doesn't include hungry pigeons. On a recent trip, we saw a large, black Muscovy duck, quite showy with his bright red wattles and the only other duck that has been successfully domesticated, beside the mallard.

Across the street is Hosp Grove, planted with 40,000 eucalyptus trees by Hosp & Partners in 1908; they hoped to make a killing by selling the trees to the Santa Fe Railroad for railroad ties. Now a city park, the grove boasts a flashy stone and mosaic sculpture, picnic tables, and streetside walking and biking trails, built by local volunteers—the beginning of a projected 12-mile trail system around Carlsbad's lagoons.

A few miles away, on Jefferson and Hill Street, is a visitor center, open Tuesday through Sunday, with some short trails through cattails leading down to the water. Watch for secretive birds like Virginia rails, soras, and moorhens.

76 BATIQUITOS LAGOON

LOCATION
Carlsbad. Access on Gabbiano Lane off Batiquitos Drive (TG1127:A7) or from Batiquitos Drive off Aviara Parkway (TG1127:D7).

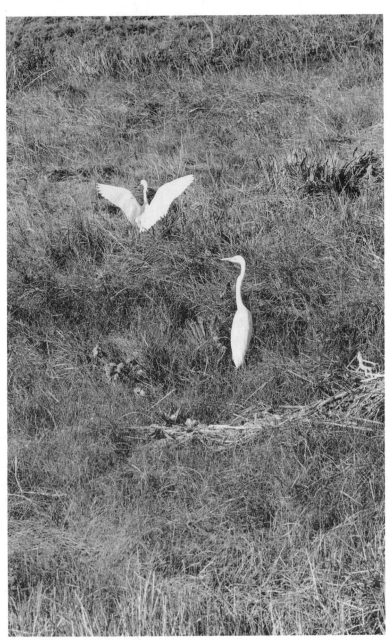

Great Egrets

DESCRIPTION

Major development has changed the upland area here, and dredging has changed the lagoon itself. Along the north shore, look for ducks, grebes, phalaropes, Bonaparte's gulls, and terns. There is a small visitor center near Gabbiano Lane.

77 SAN DIEGUITO LAGOON

LOCATION

Del Mar. Access at San Dieguito Drive and Grand Avenue (TG1187:G3).

DESCRIPTION

In this restored wetland, on the site of the old Del Mar Airport, look for osprey, kingfishers, terns, ducks, and many kinds of shorebirds.

78 FLOOD CONTROL CHANNEL

LOCATION

San Diego. Access from SeaWorld Drive and South Shores Drive (TG1268:D4).

DESCRIPTION

A roadside wildlife preserve, the channel is a good place to see ducks, egrets, herons, and shorebirds. Sometimes there are burrowing owls in the rocks, peregrine falcons flying overhead, and the uncommon little blue heron feeding in the channel.

79 FAMOSA SLOUGH

LOCATION

Loma Portal. Access at West Point Loma Boulevard and Famosa Boulevard (TG1268:B5).

DESCRIPTION

This remnant of old False Bay (now Mission Bay) is a wildlife preserve that is great for beginners, because you can see birds up close. Blue-winged teal come here every winter, and many kinds of ducks and shorebirds are usually in residence.

80 CHULA VISTA NATURE CENTER

LOCATION
Chula Vista. Park at the foot of E Street, just off I-5 (TG1309:H6). A shuttle bus runs continuously from 10:00 A.M. to 4:30 P.M. Admission fee.

DESCRIPTION
The nature center is a living wetlands museum, with interpretive trails and a walk-through slough and aviary. From its observation platforms, you can see some of the 220 bird species that visit the surrounding Sweetwater Marsh National Wildlife Refuge. Look for hawks, egrets, and shorebirds. For guided bird walks, call (619) 409-5900. Closed Mondays. For more information, check the Nature Center's website, *www.chulavistanaturecenter.org.*

Outside the Chula Vista Nature Center

Appendices

A: Native Plants of the Chaparral
B: Suggested Reading

Appendix A

NATIVE PLANTS OF THE CHAPARRAL

Drawings by Kathryn Watson

For easy reference, we've listed all entries alphabetically by common name. Latin names are included for more precise identification.

BROOM *(Baccharis sarothroides)*

Indians made brooms, brushes, and even toothbrushes out of this rough-textured shrub, which has short narrow leaves and cottony, cream-colored flowers. No relation to Scotch broom, chaparral broom usually indicates an area of disturbed chaparral, where the land was once cleared for farming or grazing cattle.

Broom

BUCKWHEAT *(Eriogonum fasciculatum)*

Once you learn to recognize its reddish-brown seed clusters, you'll see buckwheat everywhere. In spring, it's covered with pink buds and white flowers. This isn't the buckwheat that pancakes are made from, but Indians did grind the seeds into cakes and mush. A strong tea brewed from the leaves was said to cure headaches and stomach aches. Used as a mouthwash, it strengthened gums and teeth. Blossoms were steeped into a soothing eye wash.

Buckwheat

Barrel cactus

Cholla

Prickly pear

CACTI

Barrel cactus *(Ferocactus viridescens)*. Round and squat, this small cactus often grows in open areas and has yellow flowers in spring. Indians used its spines for tattoo needles.

Cholla *(Opuntia prolifera)*. The slim-branched cholla is commonly called "jumping cactus" because its joints break off easily and stick to clothes and skin. Spring flowers may be yellow or red.

Prickly pear *(Opuntia littoralis)*. The spiny flat pads of the prickly pear cactus sprout pink buds in winter, yellow flowers in spring, and red fruit in fall. The fruit is rough and prickly on the outside, but sweet inside. Watch out for the prickles; you can get a mouthful if you're not *very* careful (we speak from experience).

A cultivated variety of this cactus is cooked and served as *nopales* in Mexican restaurants. The fruits, called *tunas,* are the basis of several Mexican sweets.

In summer, prickly pear pads are covered with powdery white patches of cochineal, scale insects related to mealybugs. Female insects were collected, dried, and ground into a brilliant red dye, which, next to gold, was the most prized export from New Spain. It was used to color royal robes, tapestries, religious vestments, and the red coats of the British army.

CEANOTHUS *(Ceanothus, various species)*

Ranging in color from white to lavender blue, ceanothus, or wild lilac, has something of the look of miniature lilacs, but none of the fragrance. The common coastal variety is sometimes called popcorn bush because of the popping sound made when the seed pods burst open in summer and shoot seeds all over the ground. Indians ground the seeds into flour for mush and made mush stirrers from the wood. A wash from the leaves was used to relieve itching, especially from poison oak.

Ceanothus

CHAMISE *(Adenostoma fasciculatum)*

Nicknamed greasewood, chamise is tough on firefighters, since, like grease, it burns fast and furiously, and gives off a thick black smoke. Its name comes from the Spanish *chamiso*, a kind of crude brushwood shack that can catch fire easily. Indians used the wood for arrow shafts and throwing sticks. Tea made from the tiny needle-like leaves was said to cure tetanus, rabies, and syphilis.

Chamise

CUCUMBER, WILD *(Marah macrocarpus)*

Called "manroot" by the Indians, wild cucumber indeed has a man-sized root that is very difficult to dig up if you want to remove it from your property. Cucumber vines have a way of getting their curly tendrils around everything that grows in their vicinity. The prickly fruits are inedible, but Indians ate the seeds and used their oil as a cure for baldness. Pulverized roots were thrown into the water to stun fish and bring them to the surface for easy netting.

Wild cucumber

Laurel sumac

Lemonade berry

Manzanita

LAUREL SUMAC *(Rhus laurina)*

Since it's supposed to live only in frost-free areas, growers look for laurel sumac to determine where to plant citrus trees and avocados. The large leaves resemble bay laurel; on hot days those leaves exposed to the sun fold up to conserve water.

LEMONADE BERRY *(Rhus integrifolia)*

Lemonade berry belongs to the same family as laurel sumac and poison oak. The clusters of small pinkish "berries" you see in winter are really flowers; the sticky red fruit doesn't form until spring. A few berries dropped in a canteen can turn plain water into a lemony drink.

MANZANITA *(Arctostaphylos, various species)*

Manzanita means "little apple" in Spanish, and manzanita berries do look like tiny apples. Indians ate the fruit; pioneers turned it into cider. Some tribes made a wash from the leaves to soothe the itching of poison oak. The smooth reddish wood was carved into spoons and pipes, and its twisted burls were so prized by tourists and decorators that manzanita was in danger of extinction. Today, California law protects all species of manzanita.

MONKEYFLOWER, BUSH *(Mimulus puniceus)*

These pretty trumpet-shaped red or orange flowers may bloom anytime, but especially in the spring. Tea was brewed from the flowers, leaves, and stems to combat "Montezuma's revenge"—diarrhea.

POISON OAK *(Rhus diversiloba)*

"Leaves of three, let it be." Poison oak's three-leaf clusters are shiny green in the spring and bright red in the fall, but even in winter, with no leaves at all, it still means trouble, and touching the naked stems can give you a painful, itchy, blistering rash.

Urushiol, the oil produced by the plant, is so toxic that even inhaling the smoke from a brush fire can be dangerous. Petting an animal that has run through a patch of poison oak can be a problem too, though animals themselves don't seem to be affected, and many birds eat the berries and spread the seeds.

Certain Indian tribes managed to get along with poison oak by taking small doses of it to immunize themselves; some baked bread wrapped in its leaves and others applied the leaves to rattlesnake bites. If you think you've come in contact with it, wash the area as soon as possible with soap and water, and hope for the best.

SAGE *(Salvia, various species)*

If you smell something that reminds you of Thanksgiving, you're probably not far from a sage plant. Members of the mint family, all sages are related to the herb that flavors turkey stuffing.

Monkeyflower

Poison oak

Black Sage

White sage

Sagebrush

Scrub oak

Black sage *(Salvia mellifera),* with its dark green leaves and lavender blue flowers, is generally found along the coast. The tips can be added to salads, and the leaves can be used in cooking.

White sage *(Salvia apiana),* more common in inland areas, has large, soft, grayish leaves with small orchid-like white flowers that bees love. Indians ate the seeds, and made a tea from the leaves to treat colds and serious cases of poison oak. White sage was used in purification rituals, and also as a natural deodorant—men slept with it before a hunt to cover their human scent.

SAGEBRUSH *(Artemesia californica)*

Sagebrush, with its soft, feathery, gray-green leaves, is no relation to sage, although it does smell somewhat sagey. It's related to tarragon, absinthe, and other members of the sunflower family. Indians brewed sagebrush tea to induce menstruation and to ensure an easy childbirth and quick recovery. They also taught early settlers its usefulness as a flea repellent.

SCRUB OAK *(Quercus dumosa)*

This evergreen shrub called *chaparro,* or "shorty," by Mexican cowboys is what gives the chaparral its name. Each plant has slightly different leaves and acorns. Birds and animals seem to like the acorns well enough, but Indians ate them only in emergencies.

They preferred the bigger, sweeter acorns of the coast live oak as a staple food, and made annual treks to the mountains to gather black oak acorns, their favorite of all.

TOYON *(Heteromeles arbutifolia)*
Sometimes called Christmas berry or California holly, toyon can be recognized by its jagged leaves and bright red berries, which may appear as early as Halloween. Hollywood was named for this tall bush, which, years ago, covered its hills. Summer flowers are white, small, and unremarkable. The berries, a favorite food of birds, foxes, and other wildlife, were cooked and eaten by Indians, who also brewed a tea from the bark and leaves to use as a painkiller.

Toyon

YUCCAS
Mojave yucca (*Yucca schidigera*), or Spanish bayonet, is most common along the coast. From the center of its broad, pointed leaves, it sends up stalks that look like giant asparagus. Within weeks, they are topped with long clusters of cream-colored flowers. Indians used the tough, stringy fibers curling out of the leaves to make rope, thread, horse blankets, sandals, and baskets.

Whipple's yucca *(Yucca whipplei)*, sometimes called Our Lord's Candle, has narrower leaves, an even taller flower stalk, and finer thread-making fibers, which, during World War I, were used to make burlap. It blooms only once and then dies, while Spanish bayonet blooms year after year. Buds and seed pods were toasted and eaten by Indians.

Mojave and Whipple's Yucca

At night, flowering yuccas seem to glow in the moonlight and smell almost as sweet as night-blooming jasmine. This attracts the night-flying yucca moths that lay eggs in the flowers, and pollinate them. Each species of yucca has its own exclusive pollinator; it's a symbiotic relationship, with plant and moth dependent on each other for survival.

Bush poppy

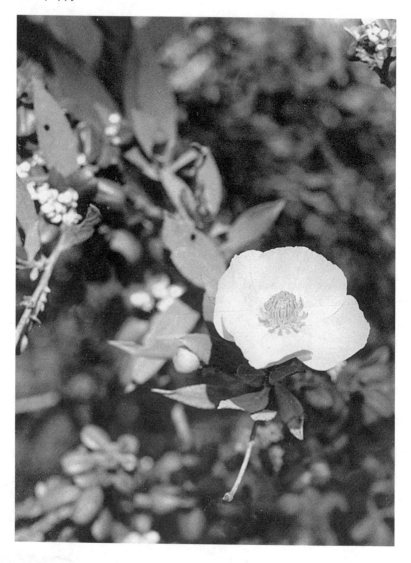

Appendix B
SUGGESTED READING

Here are some books we've particularly enjoyed. If you can't find them in your local bookstore, try museum bookshops or the public library.

GEOLOGY

Abbott, Patrick. *The Rise and Fall of San Diego.* San Diego: Sunbelt Publications, 1999.

Abbott, Patrick, and Janice K. Victoria. *Geologic Hazards in San Diego.* San Diego: San Diego Museum of Natural History, 1977.

Kern, Phillip. *Earthquakes and Faults in San Diego.* San Diego: Pickle Press, 1983.

Kuhn, Gerald, and Francis Shepard. *Sea Cliffs, Beaches, and Coastal Valleys of San Diego.* Berkeley: University of California Press, 1984.

Moore, Ellen. *Fossil Mollusks of San Diego County.* San Diego: San Diego Museum of Natural History, 1968.

HISTORY

Almstedt, Ruth. *Diegueño Curing Practices.* San Diego: San Diego Museum Papers, 1977.

Alter, Ruth. *The Painted Rocks.* San Diego: San Dieguito River Valley Regional Open Space Park Joint Powers Authority, 1995.

Carrico, Richard L. *Strangers in a Stolen Land.* San Diego: San Diego State University, Publications in American Indian Studies No. 2, 1986.

Fuller, Theodore W. *San Diego Originals.* Pleasant Hill: California Profiles Publications, 1987.

Hedges, Ken, and Christina Beresford. *Santa Ysabel Ethnobotany.* San Diego: San Diego Museum of Man, Ethnic Technology Notes No. 20, 1986.

Lee, Melicent. *Indians of the Oaks.* San Diego: San Diego Museum of Man, 1978.

Lockwood, Herbert. *Skeleton's Closet,* Vols. I and II. La Mesa: Bailey and Associates (no date).

McKeever, Michael. *A Short History of San Diego.* San Francisco: Lexicos, 1985.

Mills, James R. *San Diego, Where California Began.* San Diego: San Diego Historical Society, 1985.

Pourade, Richard, ed. *Historic Ranchos of San Diego.* San Diego: Union Tribune Publishing Company, 1969.

———, ed. *The History of San Diego,* 7 vols. San Diego: Union Tribune Publishing Company, 1960–1977.

Shipek, Florence. *The Autobiography of Delfina Cuero.* Morongo Indian
    Reservation: Malki Museum Press, 1991.
Stein, Lou. *San Diego County Place Names.* San Diego: Rand Editions,
    Tofua Press, 1975.
Ward, Mary. *Rancho de Los Peñasquitos, On the Road to Yuma.* San Diego:
    County of San Diego, Department of Parks and Recreation, 1984.

NATURAL HISTORY

Balls, Edward K. *Early Uses of California Plants.* Berkeley: University of
    California Press, 1962.
Belzer, Thomas. *Roadside Plants of Southern California.* Missoula:
    Mountain Press Publishing Co., 1984.
Berger, Wolf. *Walk Along the Ocean.* Alhambra: Border Mountain
    Press, 1976.
Clarke, Charlotte B. *Edible and Useful Plants of California.* Berkeley:
    University of California Press, 1977.
Dale, Nancy. *Flowering Plants of the Santa Monica Mountains, Coastal
    and Chaparral Regions of Southern California.* Santa Barbara: Capra
    Press, 1986.
Field Guide to the Birds of North America, Third Edition. Washington,
    D.C.: The National Geographic Society, 1999.
Head, W. S. *The California Chaparral: An Elfin Forest.* Healdsburg:
    Naturegraph Publishers, 1972.
Hinton, Sam. *Seashore Life of Southern California.* Berkeley: University of
    California Press, 1987.
Meyer, Ruth S. *Some Highlights of the Natural History* of *San Diego
    County.* Ramona: Ramona Pioneer Historical Society, 1981.
Nicol, Hank. *Notes from the Naturalist.* Del Mar: Torrey Pines Docent
    Society, 1981.
Roberts, Fred M. *The Oaks of the Southern California Floristic Province.*
    Encinitas: F. M. Roberts Publications, 1995.
Witham, Helen. *Ferns of San Diego County.* San Diego: San Diego
    Museum of Natural History, 1972.

GENERAL

California Coastal Commission. *California Coastal Resource Guide.*
    Berkeley: University of California Press, 1987.
McWilliams, Carey. *Southern California, an Island on the Land.* Salt Lake
    City: Peregrine Smith edition, 1988.
Pryde, Philip, ed. *San Diego: An Introduction to the Region.* Dubuque:
    Kendall Hunt Publishing Co., 1984.

Index

Community names appear in boldface; illustrations in italic.

About the Authors

Lonnie Burstein Hewitt has written songs for *Sesame Street*, plays for Broadway, a guidebook for writers, and hundreds of articles and reviews for the *San Diego Union-Tribune*. She leads nature/fitness walks and writes about nature in print and online.

Barbara Coffin Moore is a naturalist and environmental educator who has been leading walks through San Diego's chaparral, wetlands, beaches, and hillsides for twenty-five years. She is Program Director at the Chula Vista Nature Center and frequently writes on topics of natural history.

Between them, Lonnie and Barbara have nearly a half-century's experience walking San Diego.

Lonnie Burstein Hewitt

Barbara Coffin Moore

THE MOUNTAINEERS, founded in 1906, is a nonprofit outdoor activity and conservation club, whose mission is "to explore, study, preserve, and enjoy the natural beauty of the outdoors. . . . " Based in Seattle, Washington, the club is now the third-largest such organization in the United States, with 15,000 members and five branches throughout Washington State.

The Mountaineers sponsors both classes and year-round outdoor activities in the Pacific Northwest, which include hiking, mountain climbing, ski-touring, snowshoeing, bicycling, camping, kayaking and canoeing, nature study, sailing, and adventure travel. The club's conservation division supports environmental causes through educational activities, sponsoring legislation, and presenting informational programs. All club activities are led by skilled, experienced volunteers, who are dedicated to promoting safe and responsible enjoyment and preservation of the outdoors.

If you would like to participate in these organized outdoor activities or the club's programs, consider a membership in The Mountaineers. For information and an application, write or call The Mountaineers, Club Headquarters, 300 Third Avenue West, Seattle, WA 98119; 206-284-6310.

The Mountaineers Books, an active, nonprofit publishing program of the club, produces guidebooks, instructional texts, historical works, natural history guides, and works on environmental conservation. All books produced by The Mountaineers Books fulfill the club's mission.

Send or call for our catalog of more than 450 outdoor titles:

The Mountaineers Books
1001 SW Klickitat Way, Suite 201
Seattle, WA 98134
800-553-4453
mbooks@mountaineers.org
www.mountaineersbooks.org